WHITETAILS
IN ACTION

WHITETAILS
IN ACTION

Photography and Text
By
Mike Biggs

Jumpin' Buck Enterprises
Fort Worth, Texas

WHITETAILS IN ACTION.

Copyright © 1996 Mike Biggs

Published by:
T.P.W., Inc.
P.O.Box 330787
Fort Worth, Texas 76163
Phone 1-800-433-2102

Printed in the United States of America
First Edition

Edited by Angela Casteel, Jim Hamm

Layout and design by Mike Biggs.

Library of Congress Catalog Card Number: 96-90530

ISBN 0-9642915-2-5

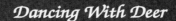

Dancing With Deer

The whitetails are wakin', it's time to get shakin'
Better hurry, don't want to be late
At the first break of morning, they come without warning
As they travel their journey with fate

They'll fill you with wonder, with plenty to ponder
They can do it without really tryin'
You'll fall prey to their magic, bring back stories so tragic
That your buddies will think that you're lyin'

They've done it for ages, sent men into rages
Over antlers that boggled the brain
They'll rattle your nerves, throw you all kinds of curves
Til your nonchalance goes down the drain

For folks in a hurry, who always must worry
Who are dancing and jumping with fear
You'll forget your concerns, as your frazzled mind learns
That you'd rather be dancing with deer

The antlers are growing, with lots of points showing
I'm hoping for drop-tines and stickers
A buck from my dreams, with long double-beams
Massive, forked tines and big kickers

Such dreams are in part, an affair of the heart
You might as well savor the view
Then get out and find him, or he'll put you behind him
He's out there, your dream could come true

There's a chance we won't find, any thing of the kind
Even so, what's important is clear
It's whitetails and friends, it's the call of the winds
But mostly it's dancing with deer

.... Mike Biggs

CONTENTS

Acknowledgements

I t's a considerable understatement to say that this work could never have been done without the help of many others. I could never overemphasize the importance of my friends. I'm really lucky to have them. It would be impossible to thank everyone who has helped along the way, but I would like to extend a special thanks to a few:

Dr. James Kroll, George & Elizabeth Jambers, Joan & J.R. Avant, Mr. & Mrs. C.W. Cain, Bud Richter, David Morris, Jeff & Tracy Avant, Tom Mantzel, Joe & Karen Langdon, Charlie Alsheimer, John Wootters, Gene Riser, Louie Schreiner, Cricket Heumann, Billy Powell, Cliff Powell, Bill Carter, Dr. Harry Jacobson, Gordon Whittington, Buddy & Tommie Lowery, David Lee, Kermit Klaerner, Jerry Smith, Lew Thompson, Jim Hamm, Tom Buckley, Dave Fulson, Mark McDonald, David & Beverly Cummings, Wyman Meinzer, Larry Tyler, Ron Henry Strait, Larry Grimland, Allen Grimland, Marc Ellett, Bob Ellett, Thompson Temple, Cecil Carder, Rodney Marsh, Bruce Williams, Kelly Snodgrass, Jack Brittingham, Glenn Sodd, the Doskocil family, Grady Allen, Tom Evans, Richard McCarty, Charly McTee, Paul Hope, Gene Fuchs, Scott & Rhonda Biggs, Gary Martin, Judd Cooney, Rusty Dawkins, Donnie Schuch, Aaron Pass, Wes Wynn, Craig Boddington, Don Keller, A.C. Parsons, Bob Cook, Jimmy Jones, Ray Sasser, Nick Gilmore, Bo & Susan Hildebrand, Betty & David Turman, Pruyn Hildebrand, Harold Jambers, Jr., Mike Love, Jack Cooper, Johnny Johnson, Bill Kinney, Bob & Tracy Hild, Cheryl Davenport, Don & Terry Pike, Joel Benavides, Ward & Sue Jones, Judy Ashworth, Brad Biggs, and Angela Casteel.

Foreword

One of nature's most generous gifts to mankind is the white-tailed deer. No inventor or scientist could ever come up with a creature more enticing or more exciting. No other woodland animal carries such an air of mystery, drama and suspense, and at the same time exudes such a feeling that things are so right in the natural world.

In their purest, most ordinary capacity, the presence of whitetails can provide humans with a feeling of calm and well-being — a soothing sense of relief, a sense that things may not be as bad as they sometimes seem. Pursuing, studying and spending time around deer will rewire your circuits, recalibrate your psyche and recharge your system.

When whitetails appear in their more exotic incarnations — giant drop-tine bucks, huge non-typicals and the like — the effects upon humans are quite remarkable. These antlers are certainly some of the most impressive sights to be seen in nature, and this fact is rarely wasted on the folks who see them. People get so excited that they practically lose their minds. Most claim *temporary* insanity, to be sure. Whitetail antlers are unique items, and big or unusual antlers tend to create a lot of enthusiasm.

No doubt there was a time in the distant, foggy, human past when most people were intimately familiar with deer. We had to be! We shared the same habitat and were even dependent upon them to some extent for food, as well as the tools and such that were made from their bones, skins and antlers. Whitetails were a part of everyday life.

Then, after thousands of years of such intimacy, the nature of humanity began to change substantially, especially in the last hundred years or so. As our ways of living have changed, and particularly as we've gravitated toward a predominantly urban society, people have begun to lose their connection to the natural world, including the deer.

Now, people are beginning to feel a profound sense of loss without that connection, and many are wanting to make it right again. One of the best ways to re-establish contact with nature and the land is by learning about whitetails and spending time in their environs. The lifestyles of deer are linked closely to the rhythms of nature. Whitetails have been a constant, dependable source of wonder throughout hundreds of generations of human lives. They're a unique piece of the human experience that should be enjoyed by everyone.

Today, people are beginning to become intimate with deer once again. We now are more technically knowledgeable about deer than ever before. Whitetails are being researched and studied by all kinds of people, and there seems to be a growing hunger for more information and more details that cannot be satisfied with the existing literature. I hope that **Whitetails In Action** will help to satisfy this need in some small way. If you'll read and enjoy the fine points of this book at a nice, slow, comfortable pace, you may find a few things that will surprise you. After all, whitetails *are* amazing.

.... **Mike Biggs**

Introduction

Not too long ago I wrote and published a book called *Amazing Whitetails*. Thousands of my whitetail images already had been published on everything from credit cards, T-shirts, catalogs and packaging, to posters, magazine covers, calendars and advertising. My work has always been well received by the public and the outdoor publishing industry. With roughly 6,000 images now published, including over 600 covers, I'm very thankful.

Even so, as a whitetail "nut" myself, I knew that I had seen and recorded events that most people had never dreamed of, let alone seen, and much of it was not being published. Most of the popular outdoor publications are businesses that operate on a "formula" basis. That is, they know what has worked for them in the past and generally don't want to stray too far from that formula. This is not necessarily a bad thing, especially if it keeps them in business. However, it does mean that most are not very willing to try dramatically new material.

So, on the one hand I'm very grateful to the outdoor press for making me one of the most published wildlife photographers in the country. On the other hand, it's very frustrating to work so hard to produce fresh, new images which are unlike any that came before, only to have publishers pass much of it over for *safer*, more ordinary material.

I was convinced that the whitetail public had become more sophisticated, better informed and quite bored with many of the current offerings. The only way to get this new material out and fill in the information gap was to become a publisher myself, and *Amazing Whitetails* was the first shot out of the barrel. The book immediately became a runaway best seller, thanks to all of you who helped to make it so. I especially want to thank the huge number of kind people who went out of their way to write and call, simply to say how much they enjoyed the book. The response was overwhelming to say the least, and I really do appreciate it.

Well, **I'M BAAACK!** — and just when you had resigned yourself to reading the regular run-of-the-mill whitetail material, again. Maybe I can help save you from all that, at least for a little while.

After the release of *Amazing Whitetails*, many people felt that it would set the standard for other deer books that followed. Some thought it would be impossible ever to match it. But I've worked long and hard, and I hope you'll be pleased with the results. *Whitetails In Action* is a unique presentation which includes exciting new concepts and remarkable new images.

Not only does *Whitetails In Action* measure up to the standard of the first book, it seeks to take that standard to another level. It includes **439 *new* color photographs**, far exceeding any other book of this nature. Many are of situations you may never have imagined, and almost all of the photos were taken **in the wild**. Included in the book are photographs of well **over 300 different bucks**, taken in over one hundred locations. There are numerous drop-tine bucks, huge non-typicals and bucks with impressive and grotesque antlers of all descriptions. *Whitetails In Action* is a brand new book with brand new material, and lots of it!

I don't believe there's ever been anything quite like this before. I think you're going to be surprised by the huge variety of impressive, interesting, bizarre and never-before-seen situations. Thanks for taking a look. I hope you'll enjoy the views.

There's nothing in the world that can kick-start a day in the woods like a big whitetail buck. Forever cautious, eminently mysterious, the mere presence of such an animal can change the whole attitude of the day — in just a few pounding human heartbeats.

DEERLY BELOVED

This is a perfect example of whitetail magic in action. The scene was an eerie, cold morning in early November, as I watched the day attempting to break through dense early morning fog. It was one of those strange, surrealistic times when the silence was deafening. I looked away for only a moment, but when I turned my head back around — he was there! And then he was gone!

People love white-tailed deer! If there is a singular truth which defines the relationship between people and whitetails, it is in that simple statement. And why not? They're more entertaining than any spectator sport, more challenging than calculus, more amazing than the window sticker on a new truck, and their mere presence lends us comfort and tranquility. They dazzle the human eye with beauty and grace, and they enrapture the human mind with the mystique that surrounds them. We love 'em, pure and simple.

Whitetails lead fascinating lives, and to study and try to understand their amazing lifestyles is to be ever more intrigued. The complexity of their seemingly "ordinary" existence is a constant source of amazement to those of us who try to figure them out. Part of the intrigue is no doubt fostered by their enigmatic presentation of

If you spend your summer days hoping to see magical sights such as this one, you'd better get an early start. Even though the day is young, these bucks will soon be bedded down for most of the day waiting for the cool respite of late afternoon. During the warmest weather, whitetails frequently bed down before sunrise and don't move around again until after sundown.

It was so late that I really couldn't see whether or not there were deer moving in the woods before me. Then, I looked up a steep oak-covered hill toward the long-past sundown to see this silhouette in the fading light.

life's realities. At times the lives of white-tails can appear so ordinary and straight-forward that it would seem that the causes and effects of their existence might be quite simple and obvious. However, just as soon as the student of whitetails digs beneath the surface, it is as though there were a great earthquake, and an avalanche of pseudo-facts and assumptions just fell into the ocean.

Whitetails are one of our best and most prominent reminders of a primordial past in which we two species helped each other down the evolutionary path, if only inad-vertently. Though their ancestors preced-ed us by a few million years, our relation-ship with deer has been ongoing for tens of thousands of years, at a minimum. They provided food for the body, challenge for the developing mind and no doubt a sense of wonder for early man's aesthetic appre-ciation. We removed the weaker or less

While we all complain heartily about the weather whenever it doesn't suit us, it's remarkable how many of the most interesting and dramatic whitetail experiences seem to take place during foul weather. Those who would wait for nice weather before traipsing out after whitetails are surely missing a major part of the whitetail romance. This photo of an old warrior standing like a ghost in the fog is a case in point.

Even whitetail bucks with small summer necks and velvet antlers carry themselves with such a noble bearing that most people can't help but be impressed by the sight.

adaptable members from their herds, shoring up their genetic aptitudes. While the relationship was far from symbiotic, the interactions of our lives have certainly helped each other along the way. We're still helping each other today in ways that aren't all that different from thousands of years ago. Whitetails are a part of the definition of our past, as well as our present.

Even though modern man's ancestors had to be deeply concerned with getting deer for food and their own survival, they nevertheless must have had great admiration for the creatures that served them so well. How could any thinking man not do so? More recently, we know that the Indians of North America greatly revered the deer, as they did the buffalo and other animals. They were grateful to the deer for furnishing them with food, clothing and

Sunrise and fog — quite a combination to emphasize a commonplace drama in the whitetail world of October. These two young bucks are sparring, practicing for a more serious day, even though they may not realize it now. They are instinctively "testing the water" and are not likely to hurt each other. However, if they meet again, perhaps two or three years later, they might well try to kill each other.

Whitetails are champion getaway artists, no matter what the terrain or the obstacle course. They can practically "fly" through tangled brush and woods, perhaps taking only seconds to cover the same distance which would take a human half an hour — if the human can get through it at all. To further magnify their abilities, they can do this just about as well in the dark as in the daytime.

tools, but even beyond that aspect they held him in the highest regard as one of nature's noble creatures. Deer were treated with great respect and admiration by the Indians and were largely regarded as equals. It was a wise perspective.

Today, we no longer look upon deer as equals. It only took a few tens of thousands of years, but we humans, intellectuals that we are, have finally stumbled upon the realization that deer are actually quite superior in most ways when encountered in a one-on-one situation in the woods. I guess we're just lucky that whitetails didn't develop opposing thumbs and larger brains. If they had, there might be deer working at computer terminals instead of people. Fortunately for humans we did have the luck of the draw where these

Whitetails are so incredibly cautious that we never even see many of them. If this buck hadn't accidentally stuck his head into the shaft of sunlight, he'd be almost impossible to see.

I was walking through the brush about noon, when I stopped to work with one of my cameras for a moment. When I looked up, this is what I saw watching me, seemingly unconcerned. You can never let your guard down, or you may miss something great. A moment later and I might not have seen him at all.

advantages are concerned. Nevertheless, we still regard whitetails with great respect and admiration. They deserve it.

After their near demise at the turn of the century due to unregulated market shooting, the whitetail comeback has been one of the biggest wildlife success stories of the twentieth century. The whitetail, as a species, owes its current existence almost entirely to the efforts of sportsmen and sportsmen's groups. Funded through the sales of hunting licenses as well as private money, these wildlife conservation efforts have brought the whitetail back from the brink of disaster. Without the huge amount of interest and financial participation by sportsmen, the whitetails might be long gone.

With current levels of interest in whitetail management at an all-time high, whitetails are certainly one of the most studied and researched animals on earth. These efforts are borne primarily out of the fact that people love deer! — and people want to know everything about this animal that fascinates them so.

It's interesting that such a wide variety of people love whitetails — from kids to old folks, businessmen, plumbers, athletes, housewives, truck drivers and engineers. Whitetails are a great equalizer in this respect. The love for deer knows no age, social or intellectual boundaries. I can think of no place more likely to harbor doctors, lawyers, mechanics, farmers, and newspaper boys, shoulder to shoulder and on an equal basis, than a deer camp or a public forest on the opening morning of deer season. The pursuit of deer, as a common purpose, brings people from many different backgrounds together, and it frequently creates long-lasting friendships in the process.

Although there are many kinds of individuals who are passionate about deer, it is quite naturally the hunters who love whitetails the most. This is true because, as a group, whitetail hunters know more about deer than other people. It's necessary that they know a great deal about whitetails in order to hunt them with *any* degree of success. Hunters spend much of their time in the woods studying and learning about the behaviors and lifestyles of deer. Further, you learn things when operating within a predator-prey relationship that you just don't learn as an outside observer. With whitetails, the more you know about them the more you want to know. And to know them is to love them.

That whitetails thrive so vigorously in today's world with its toxic environments and constantly shrinking habitat is a marvelous achievement. Their ability to adapt and deal with adversity hasn't been so challenged since the days of the market shooters. Luckily for us, they seem to be up to the challenge so far. They've learned to live in woodlots and cornfields, deep woods and open prairies. They live successfully in back yards, parks,

Hot August days bring both good news and bad news to whitetail watchers. The good news is that the antlers are about fully grown out. The bad news is that the heat will minimize whitetail movement . This was a lucky morning.

Each whitetail is a unique individual in many ways, but it's interesting how so very many of their activities seem to be carried out in unison with other deer. These three deer even seem to be walking in step with each other on a late afternoon.

Whitetails are natural born athletes. They can zig and zag and duck under or around bushes and other obstacles at incredibly high rates of speed. Their physical coordination and reaction time is unbelievable.

suburban communities and golf courses. They live on farms and ranches, on mountains, in valleys and in deserts. They cope with perhaps a 150-degree range of temperatures, considering the extremes of their northern and southwestern habitats. They have learned to survive on whatever foods are present and have adapted to eating hundreds of different food items. The whitetail motto seems to be "Make it work," and for the most part they do.

Man has always been lucky to have whitetails in his world, and we're still very fortunate in that respect. For those who are curious about their beginnings, today's whitetails can function as

Here's a sight that all whitetail watchers dream of — a monster buck leaping and bounding across an open meadow in plain sight. If you see something like this, savor the moment. Even though he may be here in mid-August, finding him won't be nearly so easy once the leaves begin to fall. With the velvet still on these extremely tall antlers, they look enormous. And they are!

a most efficient conduit, a connection to a place where our kind once lived and learned. To watch and study deer is to step through a portal in time into another, quite different world, and there is much more than deer biology to be learned by venturing into that environment. Watch closely, and if you are very alert and observant, you may catch a fleeting glimpse of yourself that you've never seen before.

I've maintained for many years that whitetails are the closest thing to real magic that most of us are ever likely to experience. Their mystique is an allure and an elusiveness which transcends all normal expectations. You can read the scientific literature about them, and pore through all the hunting books and the natural history journals. You can talk to wildlife biologists and animal researchers. You can spend hundreds or even thousands of hours in the woods observing them, studying them, taking notes and making comparisons. But none of this is likely to explain to you just where that big buck came from (the one that appeared out of nowhere, as though from a puff of smoke), or where he went when he disappeared (after all, he only stepped behind the one small bush but never emerged from the other side). Big bucks can make rabbits-out-of-hats tricks look so easy. It's no wonder people love whitetails so much.

Pay close attention to fencelines when traveling in whitetail country. After fences have been in place for a period of time, they begin to define some of the travel corridors that whitetails will use on a regular basis. Many times you will find visible deer trails next to the fences. Also, regular crossings can be found. Wait there and you might see something really exciting — like this!

Sometimes fence crossings seem to be in very logical places, such as where the fence might be broken or sagging. Other times crossings will seem to be at very arbitrary spots on long, nondescript stretches of fence. Even so, you'll frequently see deer such as this one cross at the very same nondescript spot time after time, day after day, and sometimes year after year.

For most antler lovers, it just doesn't get much better than a super-wide, heavy-antlered, triple-drop-tine buck. Drop-tines have been the subject of much conversation and debate. They are likely a result of genetic heritage in many cases, but some may be caused by other factors such as injury. Drop-tines are more prevalent among older bucks.

HEAVENLY HEADBONES

Whitetail headbones have caused many a human heart to pound. There's just something about the unique nature of antlers that makes people crazy. Antler enthusiasts are a little like gold prospectors. When they find a really big or unusual antler, either on the ground or on the deer, it's much like a prospector finding gold. Unique and unusual antlers are treasured by many people.

The Middle English term was *auntelers*. In Old French the word was *antoilliers*. In Latin they were called *anteocularis*. The American Heritage Dictionary now calls them *antlers*. We may call them antlers, or by any of a large number of colloquialisms, including racks, horns, crowns, hatracks, buckhorns, headbones and others. No matter what we choose to call them, it's more than likely that the word will be spoken in an emotional context ... perhaps reverently, maybe fervently,

passionately for sure. Whitetail antlers are the things that dreams are made of.

It's true that people can get excited over seeing an antlerless deer. But, if you want to see some real, unadulterated, big-time enthusiasm, just watch a truly large buck walk out in front of a human. It's amazing the amount of excitement that whitetails with big antlers can generate. Quite frankly, people in general and deer hunters in particular have a tendency to just go nuts in the presence of a big deer. Buck fever is an amazingly universal experience.

These are the kinds of bucks that dreams are made of. The buck on the left is one of the most beautiful typical-antlered bucks I've ever seen, and the buck above is a monster non-typical.

It goes beyond the logical configuration of a person simply being "surprised" or "amazed" by something unexpected. It's much more than just a surprise. It reaches a deeper level than that. Let someone get a glimpse of a big 12-pointer with a drop-tine, and nine times out of ten they're over the top. They couldn't be more enthusiastic if they'd just had a close personal encounter with aliens from outer space.

It's interesting how much human emotion can be mustered just by laying eyes on some gnarly, oversized headbones. It creates an adrenaline rush somewhat like the experience of a near-miss rattlesnake strike, or perhaps like a close call with a scorpion. It's certainly much more pleasant, but it tends to cause a more or less "desperate" level of excitement just the same. I'm sure you get the idea. Given the fact that you're reading this book you've probably experienced the concept.

The allure of antlers has been around for thousands of years. Antlers have always carried a powerful fascination for many people. Nobody knows for sure when it all began, but it was a long time ago. No doubt early man used bones as tools and weapons, and one can almost visualize one of those early humans on the day he picked up an antler instead of a leg bone. It's easy to imagine that the expression on his face may well have changed from one of boredom or seriousness to one of wonder and curiosity as he felt the texture and examined the shape of the antler. Who knows what might have gone through his mind? Just imagine the gyrations that his thought processes must have been going through,

These two outstanding non-typicals would rattle the nerves of even the most jaded antler enthusiast. Heavy mass, multiple drop-tines, sticker-points, forks, widespread, long tine-length — between the two of them, they just about have it all.

This buck had already dropped both of his antlers by early January when this photo was taken. Some bucks in the same area probably held their antlers for as much as an additional four to six weeks. Different bucks shed their antlers at different times, depending on individual health and other factors.

In late February, this buck had already shed one antler. When I saw him again eight or nine days later, he was still wearing one antler. Sometimes antlers are shed together, but many times they are dropped at different times and places.

seeing the antler on the ground, now in his hand — perhaps recalling a recent sighting of a deer with antlers on his head.

Now, as then, antlers remain one of nature's most awe-inspiring artifacts. If you personally picked up a big shed antler right now, I wouldn't be surprised if the look on your face was somewhat similar to the look I imagined in the last paragraph.

The facts about antlers are just about as amazing as their "magical" properties. The composition of antlers show them to be true bone rather than the keratin-sheath-type growths of animals with "horns." The very idea that a buck drops his antlers every year and then regrows them completely from scratch is hard for some people to believe, but of course it's true. The

Antlers begin re-forming generally about the first of May and grow like wildfire through the summer, particularly during the months of June and July. The group of deer at the top of the page was photographed in mid-June. The photos of the buck at the bottom of the page (and both photos are of the SAME buck) show the incredible amount of antler growth that takes place in just a little over 100 days. The photo on the left was taken about May 10, and the shot on the right was taken about September 1.

The buck in the lower left picture was photographed in mid-June and the bucks above were seen in early July. This is the time that antlers are growing most rapidly. It's an amazing time.

fact that this is accomplished in just a little over 100 days makes antlers the fastest growing bones in the world. There's no really good analogy for this process. In terms of the relative amount of bone grown, it might be a little like watching a baby human grow from the size of a new-born to the size of a six-year-old — in only a three or four month period.

In order for whitetail bucks to perform this miraculous feat, they must beg, borrow and steal from the rest of their body. Much of their nutritional intake is spent on the production of antlers. During the time of maximum antler growth and hardening, a whitetail buck's body is actually transferring calcium from the skeletal system to the antlers, because it's simply not possible for a buck to ingest enough calcium through the regular dietary process. That's why it's so important that bucks maximize

The four photos above chronicle several months in the life of one buck. They were taken about one month apart — early June, early July, early August, and early September. As you can see, summer is a very dynamic time for whitetail bucks. This buck was believed to be approximately three years old at the time this series was taken.

The buck in these two photos is the same one as in the series at the top of the page — but these were taken the NEXT YEAR. The picture on the left was taken in early July and the one on the right was taken in early August. One year's maturity made a considerable difference in the size and character of this buck's antlers.

These three photos of the same buck were taken during a relatively short period of time. The photo at the top left was taken on June 26, the bottom right photo was taken on July 14 and the large center photo was taken August 15. At the time of the last photo his antlers were fully grown and just beginning to dry out and harden. The tips of his beams very nearly touched.

When summer begins to fade into fall, whitetail antlers begin to look a little fuzzier as they start drying out. Bucks look very impressive this time of year with their full-grown antlers still in velvet. All the bucks on this page are probably getting very near the time when they will strip off their velvet.

their intake of nutrients during this period. In fact, though it is not widely recognized, the antler-growing period can be dangerous to a buck that is in poor health or in an environment that does not supply enough food. Some bucks actually die during this "summer-stress" period.

After having shed their antlers in late winter or early spring, most bucks do survive the rigorous demands of antler regeneration. In the majority of situations, by the time that late summer arrives, most bucks appear to be fat and happy, and their antlers are essentially full-grown. After the complete calcification and hardening of the antlers takes place (and the

When the velvet finally comes off it is as though the bucks have been transformed overnight, both in terms of physical appearance and attitude. I surprised the buck at the upper left just before sunrise. He was vigorously thrashing his velvet off on a tree limb and had leaves and branches tangled in the torn, bloody velvet strips. The other two are freshly cleaned.

The photo above illustrates at least two interesting points. First, all bucks do not shed their velvet at precisely the same time. There is generally about a one-month span of time in which the various individual bucks in an area will shed their velvet. The other point illustrated here is the role of genetics in the formation of antlers. It would be hard to imagine that these two bucks are not very closely related.

days begin to shorten) the velvet is removed in one fashion or another. It's possible in some cases to see a buck in full, smooth velvet disappear into the woods for 30 minutes to an hour and reappear with clean, bony antlers and no trace of velvet or blood whatsoever. Some, however, are not quite so efficient. It's common to see bucks with shreds of velvet hanging from one or both antlers. They sometimes leave the shreds hanging like that for several days. In a few instances I've seen bucks that removed the velvet from only one antler, leaving the other antler

All bucks don't remove their velvet in exactly the same fashion. There are a lot of variations. Some clean their antlers completely in an hour's time. Others are bloody for a full day or even two. A few bucks strip off each side on different days. Some individuals don't bother to remove pieces of it for weeks, letting the dried shreds hang on indefinitely.

sheathed in velvet for several days before removing it as well. I've even seen a couple of mature, dominant bucks with velvet shreds hanging right through the duration of the rut. The variety in the performance of this cyclical task points out the individuality of whitetail bucks. The more you observe and learn about whitetails, the more you begin to realize that there is a great deal of individuality among deer.

While there may still be some controversy as to the "purpose" of antlers, it seems apparent that there are several purposes. They function as a social status symbol to some extent, although the buck with the largest antlers is not necessarily the "top dog." They're used in "warning" postures, and when necessary, they are wielded as offensive weapons in the serious battles for the determination of social standing. If they had evolved primarily as a defensive

Here are some very good typical-antlered bucks. The buck at the top of the page is an extremely rare 7x7 typical. After having seen thousands of bucks, I've only seen four or five 7x7's. The buck at the bottom is a very symmetrical 5x5.

mechanism, whitetail does would also be antlered, but, with rare exceptions, that is not the case. They're frequently utilized as back-scratchers and tummy-rubbers. They are also used to make the all-important buck rubs, to advertise presence, territoriality or dominance. It's possible, maybe even probable, that whitetail bucks display their antlers as a sexual attractant — much the same way that brightly colored male birds use their colors to attract potential mates. It's curious to note that we have no idea as to what characteristics a whitetail doe might prefer in terms of antlers. Do you suppose tall is better, or perhaps wide? I wonder if the number of points or the amount of mass makes any difference. It's an odd situation in that no matter which buck a doe might prefer — the

These are outstanding typicals. The buck at the upper right is a really nice 6x6 typical with an extra sticker point. He held his head proudly as though he were royalty. As far as I could tell, he was the "king" of the area. The buck at the bottom of the page has a well-developed 6x7 typical frame. While 6x7's are not as rare as 7x7's, they're still very scarce.

Here is a picture of near-perfection, but only if you like really big, extremely symmetrical, typical antlers. I was slipping along the edge of a brushline when a smudge in the fog materialized into this magnificent buck. The sun was trying to shine through the dense early morning fog, and everything was dripping wet. There was not a hint of wind or noise. The buck seemed to be more apparition than reality as he moved silently toward some unknown destination. The moment was brief but remarkable.

This wary buck has a very large 5x5 typical mainframe with several sticker points. Really big, purely typical bucks are rare because bucks that are capable of growing that kind of size and mass usually grow some extra or abnormal points.

largest bodied, most aggressive bucks will likely be the ones doing the breeding.

The fact that whitetail antlers come in such a wide variety of shapes and sizes, and with so many individual peculiarities, is a very endearing factor where humans are concerned. People are such "collectors" of things, particularly things unique, unusual, rare or impressive. And what could possibly meet all of these criteria any better than a huge set of whitetail antlers. Truly big and unusual antlers are far more rare than diamonds or gold, and they are collected and coveted accordingly.

I'm not going to get into the very basic "nuts and bolts" about how, when and why antlers are formed, grown and shed, because I've already done that in my book "Amazing Whitetails." Suffice to say that antlers are dropped in the winter or early spring, are regrown entirely from the pedicels over roughly a 100 to 120 day period, and then the velvet covering is removed and the antlers are polished. It's truly an amazing process. There's nothing else like it in the world.

I can't imagine that there could be many subjects that have been researched and studied as much as the phenomenon of whitetail antlers. Yet, with all the incredible amount of attention they receive, there still is a great deal of uncertainty about many of the various nuances of antler development and growth. It often seems that there are more exceptions than there are rules.

Most of us know that there are three primary factors which, incorporated together, will largely determine a given animal's antler producing potential. **Genetics, nutrition and age** are the big three. They each contribute mightily to the equation, but there are obviously other more subtle variables which also come into play, particularly where non-typical antlers are concerned. And even though there is so much information floating around about genetics, nutrition and age, there still is considerable uncertainty as to just exactly how any particular individual animal will be affected by different combinations of these factors.

Wildlife managers throughout the country are trying all kinds of different approaches in their efforts to grow whitetails with bigger and more interesting antlers. They are experimenting with a wide variety of different

This is an unusual buck. He has very heavy beams and an impressive 6x6 typical frame with an extra brow tine. As you can see, he has a very small neck. The small neck was a little confusing, since the rut was in full swing. As it turned out, he was taken by a hunter about a month later. He had virtually no teeth, and was perhaps as much as 10 years old, or more.

techniques on such basic issues as habitat improvement, supplemental feeding, population control and age structure. Certainly, progress is being made, but rarely is the outcome very predictable, other than to say that the overall quality of the herd will be improved. In almost all programs which apply generally accepted whitetail management principles, the quality of the overall herd is *noticeably* improved. The *averages* (of weights, points, spreads, scores, etc.) are improved considerably. The *bottom* levels are definitely raised, and that alone will raise the averages. However, the top end of the bell curve is harder to move. Improvements will be seen, and some exceptional animals will be produced, but on a fairly unpredictable basis in most

*The mature 12-point buck at the left has a substantial drop-tine on his right side. The buck below has fewer points, but the wide spread and sweeping beams, coupled with matching **double drop-tines,** make him a very impressive sight.*

No book of mine would be complete without at least one photograph of the above buck. This is the buck I call "Ol' Dropkick." He's certainly one of the most interesting bucks I've ever seen. I was able to get this quick shot of the buck on the right as he pranced across a small clearing. Although he has 12 points, his drop-tine is easily his longest tine.

cases. It's been quite frustrating for some game managers.

I've worked on a very large number of different ranches that have intensive whitetail management programs, and all have definitely improved the quality of their deer. Yet, the concept of intentionally growing incredible "super-bucks" with any kind of regularity or true predictability has simply not come to pass.

It's interesting to note an experience that I had just recently. The experience is quite notable

This velvet buck has massive antlers with double drop-tines close in on the beams. He has several pounds of antlers on his head. It must get tiresome carrying all that weight around.

Quite frequently (relatively speaking) you see drop-tines which are very close in on the beam. It seems that this one might very well impede his vision on his left side.

This is a small-bodied deer, but he carries a handsome set of antlers, including a notable drop-tine. As you can tell, he's already seen me. He flew like the wind just after this shot.

I only got a brief peek through the brush at this massive triple drop-tine buck. I tried to find and photograph him a number of other times, but for the most part he simply outsmarted me.

because it fits a pattern which I've seen repeatedly. While working on several different "managed" ranches located in one particular area, I saw some very good quality bucks and a few exceptional ones. Shortly thereafter, I spent some time (in the same area) on some "unmanaged" properties where the habitat was poor, the deer were over-populated, and there was a shortage of nutritional foods. *Twice*, during the times when I was working on the

The double drop-tine buck at the upper right is very impressive with 16 or 17 points. I waited patiently for several days at a waterhole blind, and he finally showed up. He was actually too close (perhaps 20 yards) for the big 500mm lens I was using, and I was lucky to get this picture. The big deer at the bottom is the buck I call "Amber-Eyes." He is beautiful, dominant and in his prime.

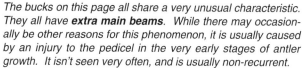

*The bucks on this page all share a very unusual characteristic. They all have **extra main beams**. While there may occasionally be other reasons for this phenomenon, it is usually caused by an injury to the pedicel in the very early stages of antler growth. It isn't seen very often, and is usually non-recurrent.*

more marginal properties, I saw monster bucks. They were the *two* best bucks that I saw throughout the entire region. Of course this doesn't prove anything. It only serves to point out an all too common example that I've seen many times over the years. It seems that *truly* exceptional or unusual bucks tend to be freaks of nature that are as yet somewhat beyond our understanding, much less our control. They tend to show up at unpredictable, unexpected times and places, frequently with no apparent regard for quality of habitat, nutritional availability or local genetic propensities. It's a part of the mystery that keeps us going. Just about every time we think that we've unraveled the antler puzzle, more aberrations appear.

Nevertheless, people everywhere, from scientists to good ol' boys, are continuing to study the whitetail antler phenomenon.

Whitetail bucks sometimes grow bifurcated or "forked" tines similar to those that mule deer grow. There may be only one fork or there may be matched forks on both sides. One or two forks is relatively common, but occasionally there are bucks with three or four. It is most likely a hereditary trait, and bucks which show this characteristic usually will grow some variation of the pattern year after year.

It would almost be a shame if the questions were ever answered completely. Just look at all the people it would put out of work, not to mention the effect it might have on our romance with the mystery of whitetail antlers. Then again, most of us are so infatuated with the romance that it would probably have no effect at all.

Where the admiration of whitetail antlers is concerned, there are two primary classifications, fostering two different schools of thought when preferences are considered. What I'm referring to here is the differentiation of antlers into "typical" and "non-typical" categories. "Typical" antlers are generally considered to be "normal" antlers, which infers a basic sameness from one animal to the next. Purely typical antlers would normally have beams that sweep up, out and

As you have already seen, there are many variations of non-typical antlers — sticker points, drop-tines, forked tines, double-beams, and so on. One type of antler conformation which is quite scarce as well as very appealing is a non-typical rack that has a "typical" look. Even though there may be a considerable amount of non-typical features, the overall rack is more or less symmetrical from side to side. The two bucks on this page fit this description. They are both extremely large, with numerous extra points, but they still have a "typical" look.

forward, and all of the points would be mainly upright and in-line on the beams. This is the basic architecture of whitetail antlers. Far and away, the majority of whitetail bucks do seem to grow "typical" antlers, especially in their younger years. In fact, large numbers of bucks in many areas grow nothing but smooth, typical antlers throughout their entire lives. As many wildlife managers and ranchers have learned, *eight-point typicals* are easily the most common whitetail bucks on the planet, when bucks two years of age or older are considered. When you watch whitetails as much as I do, it's

Here are some of the most unusual brow tines that you're likely to see. They're very long, bladed and split into multiple points. He has 18 scorable points and a few more bumps.

The right antler is quite normal with one of the tines forked. The left antler doesn't match at all and gives him a very lopsided appearance. The left pedicel was probably injured.

This buck appears to have TWO sets of brow tines ...or perhaps the extras are just matched upside-down drop-tines. He also has a distinctive face with white circles around his eyes.

Talk about weird! This gnarly-antlered buck has crooked double drop-tines, monstrous brow tines, poorly defined beams and extra points. There's no telling what caused such a conglomeration.

47

Just about everybody loves a wide-antlered buck. This 12-pointer just emerged from the woods, and now he's heard my shutter click. His antlers are about 26" wide inside the beams.

fact. I've heard several believable stories about such animals. Even so, it's safe to say that "typical" antlers carrying anything more than six-by-six points would be quite "non-typical" in terms of their rarity.

While there are exceptions, very young whitetail bucks almost always have typical antlers with two to twelve points. Even though many bucks grow up to be "typicals for life," or even "eight-pointers for life," there are some great exceptions. Bucks which have the capability of growing very large and/or massive antlers, rarely continue to grow *purely* typical antlers, once they have reached maturity. When a whitetail buck begins to develop an unusually large volume of bone on his head, part of the excess almost invariably is channeled into

This buck doesn't have all that many points but who cares? At perhaps 27" wide, with fairly good tine-length and mass, he is a very impressive animal. I surprised him as he walked over the top of this hill in the rain on a cold winter day.

almost possible to get a little jaded and bored with the "plain vanilla" eight-pointers. Almost, but not quite! Even among the legions of eight-pointers, there is a tremendous variety in terms of antler size, shape, mass, spread and height, not to mention other factors such as the individual personalities of the deer. There's more than enough to keep you occupied.

There are also many typical-antlered bucks which are not eight-pointers. They can range anywhere from two-pointers to perhaps 18-pointers. The most extreme examples that I've actually seen in the woods include a few seven-by-seven typicals and one five-by-eight, but I have no doubt that eight-by-eight's and nine-by-nine's are certainly a possibility, if not a some form of non-typical growth, something such as "sticker-points" or "kickers" at the very least. That's why the record books are filled with so many non-typicals which score higher than the No. 1 world-record "typical." Anytime a whitetail buck has the capability of producing a world-class set of antlers, the resulting growth almost always includes some non-typical characteristics. From that perspective, a really huge set of typical antlers may not be as unique as a giant non-typical rack, but it may be much rarer.

If you happen to agree with the old saying that "variety is the spice of life," then you'll be wanting to thank your lucky stars for the existence of non-typical antlers. While it may be true

When the question arises as to whether or not a buck's antlers are very massive, the answer is usually easy to discern. The two bucks at the bottom of the page are instantly perceived as "massive," as opposed to the thin-antlered buck at the top of the page. The "pencil-horned" buck at the top and the lower-left buck each have 14 points. The number of points just doesn't tell the story.

Tall-antlered, or "high-horned" bucks are real attention getters, especially when the tines begin to reach 14 or 15 inches like the bucks on this page. Antlers this tall are quite rare, probably as rare as drop-tines, maybe even more so.

that typical antlers have more than enough variety to make life with whitetails interesting, the non-typical concept raises the ante by several levels. What *would* we do without sticker-points, drop-tines, double-brows, kickers, extra beams, forked tines, hooks, and just good ol' heavy, gnarly antlers. These things are the spice of whitetail life, and to see or own such things would be at the top of the aspirations list for most whitetail enthusiasts.

Once again, whitetails overwhelm us with mystery when it comes to understanding the causes of the antler aberrations which make up the "non-typical" mix. Some examples can be explained as "hereditary," or "caused by injury," but the causes

Even though beam-length is difficult to judge in the field, there are rare times when long length is fairly obvious. Look at the beam-lengths on these two bucks! Both are long-beamed and very wide. The buck on the right is also extremely massive. Bucks like these will make you shake in your boots. The length of the beams in the left photo may be about 25" to 27". The beam-lengths in the right photo are perhaps in the 28" to 30" range. There is no particular length that is considered "normal," but about 18" to 22" is common.

for some growth patterns can't be defined quite so conveniently. For instance, what about the bucks that grow drop-tines, but only part of the time. Some bucks have drop-tines every year of their lives (very rare), while others grow them only once and then revert to smooth beams thereafter. Some bucks skip back and forth with drop-tines coming and going almost every other year. Most attempts to predict drop-tine development end up in confusion and frustration. About the only thing that seems overwhelmingly true about drop-tines is that they are definitely more prevalent among older, more mature deer. This does not mean that age causes drop-tines. However, many bucks that do have the capability of growing such points do not show this quality until they are fully

mature. When a buck grows a drop-tine, it often happens for the very first time (or the only time) at an advanced age.

Further, bucks which grow drop-tines, sticker-points or forked-tines are frequently inconsistent. The relative sizes, positions and proportioning of these aberrations change from year to year. Some bucks grow non-typical antlers every year, but the odd points may move around on the typical portion of the rack from one year to the next. All things considered, trying to predict the growth patterns of non-typical whitetails is a little like trying to predict a winning lottery number. However, for most of us, it's infinitely more rewarding.

LEAPS & BOUNDS

A whitetail's physical prowess is one of his most amazing attributes. Few animals can match the pure grace and simplicity of a whitetail on the move. The buck above glides effortlessly over rough ground, creeks and obstacles as he hurries toward the sound of rattling antlers. He was "all ears" as you can see. When a buck is focused like that, it is as though his legs are put on "automatic pilot."

Some people dream of flying like a bird. Perhaps the better dream would be to possess the agility and grace of a whitetail. For that matter, there are times when you'd swear that a whitetail *can* fly. A whitetail in motion is a shockingly beautiful thing. Whether you're watching a heavy-bodied buck powering his way beyond the limits of your visibility, or marveling at a dainty-footed doe as she sails over a shoulder-high fence, you can't help but be impressed with the exquisite combination of grace and strength. The energy is channeled so smoothly, so precisely.

Whitetails are natural-born athletes. After only a few days, newborn fawns are easily making ten-foot leaps. All this athletic ability is the product of millions of years of evolution. There may have been a time when whitetails (or their predecessors) were slow or clumsy, but not lately.

This drop-tine buck has a tail like an ostrich plume and he's using it to full advantage. There were some other deer in sight that I had not yet spooked, but he took them all with him when he panicked and fled. He was out in an open area when he heard my camera shutter snap, and he was none too pleased about it. That was the last time I ever saw him.

Here is another buck which is on the fly, literally. In stark contrast to the buck at the top of the page, this buck appears to have a bobbed tail. He's a large-bodied, wide-antlered eight-pointer. I was walking quietly through some heavy brush when he came whistling past me, about three feet off the ground and about 20 yards to my right. I never did see what he was running from.

This tall-antlered buck should have gotten flight clearance from the nearest air traffic control tower. I had been slipping down a fencerow on a hot August morning when I saw him standing in the shade at the edge of a field. When I tried to get closer he saw me and immediately left for parts unknown. He really doesn't seem to be putting out much effort to make this incredibly high and long leap.

The predators of those earlier times naturally selected the slow and the clumsy and ate them for breakfast, lunch and dinner until there were no more of them. The quicker, stronger, more agile members of the species have survived and reproduced, ultimately producing the whitetail athletes that we know today. The moves that we consider so amazing, whitetails take for granted. These abilities are an integral part of their being.

As far as I know, the limits of their physical abilities have never been tested or measured scientifically, but perhaps those facts don't really matter too much. There's little doubt that whitetails can leap eight or nine foot fences; they can probably hit 40 miles per hour in a pinch; and a 30 to 40 foot broad

I was walking over a hill late one morning when I accidentally startled this buck. He was apparently bedded down under a cedar bush, and neither of us saw the other until I was very close. He turned inside-out.

jump is certainly within their reach. It's not really the distances, or the heights, or the actual speeds which are so impressive in and of themselves. What makes it all so impressive is the *style* with which these feats are performed — smooth as silk and graceful as a ballet dancer. It's enough to make you want to stand up and applaud.

I have watched, studied and pursued whitetails for many years, and I've always had a great appreciation for their abilities. However, when I began to concentrate on photographing deer extensively, that appreciation was expanded even more. I began to notice little things and pay more attention to details. For example, anyone who has ever watched a whitetail jump

The buck on the left is coming over a fence directly toward my waterhole blind. He stood up vertically and simply hopped over — nothing to it! The buck below shows the ease with which whitetails cover rough ground. I had been watching him from my position in a creek bed. When I moved he saw me and made a graceful exit from my neck of the woods.

I watched this handsome buck late one fall afternoon as he traveled from a bedding area to a feeding area. He had no idea I was hiding in my blind in the brush. He either did not hear the camera (unlikely) or ignored it and went on his merry way.

over a fence knows what a beautiful sight it is. It's such a smooth, graceful moment that, although I had never really thought about it much in those terms, it always seemed to be a relatively "slow-motion" movement. Then, I began trying to photograph deer making these jumps. The whole process of trying to get such photos is fraught with problems and is rarely successful, but I've learned a lot during the hundreds of hours that I've sat, concealed along fencelines, watching deer that occasionally actually jumped the fence. One of

the bits of information I discovered was that my perception of a whitetail's jump as being a slow-motion movement was entirely wrong. It may seem trivial, but for this type of photography, timing is everything, and the minute amounts of time involved in an "ordinary" jump were astounding to me. The motor drives on my cameras are capable of shooting photos at approximately five frames per second. That sounds like it should be plenty, doesn't it? But it's not really, not for fence-jumping photos anyway. Basically, I found that I can only

It's always a very exciting event to see a group of bucks running together. I surprised this foursome as I came out of some heavy brush at the edge of a food plot. It's hard to say whether they were grouped together simply because they had all come individually to the oat patch, or because it was early fall and they were still running together as a bachelor group.

That's no jump for a show-dog ...or deer. He sailed over the relatively tall fence like it was no big deal. He obviously could've jumped much higher. There are many reliable reports of whitetail bucks jumping eight-foot fences.

get a maximum of three frames of a deer jumping a fence ... *and that's only six-tenths of a second!* Generally that means that in the first frame the deer's hind legs will still be on the ground or just dragging off. In the second frame the deer will be straddling the fence, and in the third frame the deer's front feet will be touching down, or very nearly so. Only twice have I *ever* gotten four frames in sequence of a whitetail jumping a fence. The series on page 52 is one example. I guess I just never realized what a long time a second can be until I began looking at it from this perspective. It certainly illustrates how important it is that a photographer's reflexes and photographic timing be on the mark.

Of course this doesn't even take into account that the photographer must also get the deer in focus at the moment of the jump, and further, that the focus changes during the jump. As previously mentioned, the whole process of trying to take good jumping-deer photos is fraught with problems. But sometimes it works!

Another interesting aspect of the fence-jumping abilities of deer is the extremely efficient conservation of energy that they practice, even as they make spectacular leaps. Have you ever noticed how, almost without fail, whitetails just barely seem to make it over the fence? I've been asked over and over again, when people have looked at my various jumping photos, "Did he make it over? It looks like he may not quite make it." With extremely few exceptions, they do make it over, but usually with no room to spare. It would be a waste of precious energy resources to put anything more into the jump than was required, and whitetails have become very, very skilled at judging exactly the amount of energy necessary. Once in a great while, a deer will miss on his attempt to clear a fence or other obstacle. I've only seen it a couple of times, and it was a startling thing to see. You just don't expect to see a graceful whitetail go head over heels into the dirt. It happens, but such an occurrence is apparently rare. There have also been a very few times when I've seen a deer actually "over-shoot" a fence so much that it was comical, but again, not very often.

One unfortunate situation that I've seen a number of times is a deer that has caught its hind legs in the top two strands of a wire fence while attempting a jump. These deer didn't actually misjudge the *height* of the fence. They jumped plenty high enough to get over the top. The problem seems to lie primarily with a major misjudgment in timing. They brought their back legs forward an instant too soon,

When a monster whitetail like this one comes flying over a fence, those front legs fold up just like a bird in flight. He's just a short hop and about a half second from the other side.

Even though whitetails may jump logs, bushes, fences and tall buildings with ease, there are rare occasions when the picture does not appear quite as graceful, sometimes even comical. Once in a great while, a deer will not quite clear the top of an obstacle, and will go head over heels into the dirt. I've only seen it a very few times and it was a startling thing to see, given the usual expectations when watching a whitetail jump. Even though they may sometimes seem a little ungainly and off-balance like the two deer at the top of the page, they are usually right on the mark and literally "fly" over ...like the two examples at the bottom of the page. Those two are shooting over like streamlined projectiles.

These two bucks must have gone to the same school. It's remarkable how similar their postures and positions over the fence appear. They look a little like kangaroos. The two pictures were taken at different times and different places. I had seen the buck on the left about two months earlier and he was a full-fledged 10-pointer at that time. He now has broken off four points — both brow tines and both forks, one off each primary tine. The buck on the right also has broken off two points in the time since I had seen him about one month previously. To point out their physical individuality, their facial features are quite different, as is their coloration.

placing their hooves between the top two strands of wire on the approach side of the fence. Their legs caught on the second wire, and the two strands instantly twisted together, dooming the whitetail. It's always a shame and a difficult thing to see. There's a chance that their poor depth perception may play a part in these tragedies.

We know, both from research and from practical experience, that whitetails have poor depth perception. I don't know how many times I've been caught in the open by whitetails, yet, as long as I've remained perfectly motionless, they rarely have been able to pick me out from the background, even at extremely close ranges. Almost everyone who has spent much time with deer has had many similar experiences.

This obvious difficulty that whitetails have with depth perception would seem to be a real problem where running and dodging is concerned. Perhaps it is, but if so, it's a problem that they've overcome with flying colors. As we all know, they are very

When whitetails are startled, they have both the means and the ability to remove themselves very expeditiously from any danger, real or imagined. I sneaked up behind the buck in the upper left corner as he fed in a large oat field. I was quite close when he noticed me and you can see that he strained every muscle in his body to get away ASAP. The other two bucks here were equally motivated.

In their pursuit of freedom from uninvited guests and other predatory types, whitetails are rarely deterred by heavy brush or thick woods. It seems that they "fly" through the thickest tangles just about as easily as they do the wide open spaces. The buck in the timber above is traveling mostly about three or four feet above the ground ...and at just less than the speed of sound.

capable when it comes to covering uneven ground in a hurry. Actually, that's somewhat of an understatement. One of the most exciting experiences in the world is a firsthand opportunity to watch a scared whitetail put three hundred yards of rough, uneven, tangled space between you and himself. It's poetry in motion, lightning fast and smooth as butter. Further, it's always amazing to me that the very same three hundred yards that took the deer only seconds to cover, can easily take a human 20 minutes or more. In some cases, it's essentially impossible for the human to cover the same ground at all, in *any* amount of time. And it's no small thing that whitetails are able to put on these performances in low light or at night with the same sort of accuracy. It's very impressive.

That whitetails can perform in this manner with such poor depth perception is remarkable. They have more than overcome their shortcoming with an extremely well-developed sense of touch, along with an ability to react so quickly that it almost defies normal comprehension. Their tactile abilities are so sensitive that, even as they are running and dodging, they are instantly and instinctively able to determine the nature of the surface where a hoof is landing. Their reaction time is so fast that they are instantaneously making corrections on the fly as they go. It's not a perfect world, and they occasionally slip and fall, but not very often. Even when that happens, they right themselves so quickly that a casual observer may not even realize that they ever went down.

Sometimes, when whitetails are frightened, but not extremely so, they will run with a "prancing" gait. At times it seems that they are using the "prancing" posture as a warning to other deer, much in the same way that they wave their white flags.

Whether they are jumping fences, throwing up a roostertail of dust as they shoot across an open pasture, or boring through a tangled forest at warp speed, whitetails in action are always exciting to see. Such sights can transform ordinary citizens into whitetail "nuts" on the spot. These outrageous displays of power and precision may be brief, but the memories which they produce are guaranteed to last a lifetime.

A whitetail's overall physical prowess is one of his most amazing attributes. Whitetails are powerful, yet smooth in their actions. They are incredibly accurate in their moves, yet they move with such style. They are extremely efficient in their expenditure of energy and resources, yet dazzling as they perform their tasks efficiently. Few animals can match the pure grace and simplicity of a whitetail on the move.

The monster 10-pointer above has just galloped across a small clearing and is leaning into the turn as he ducks around a clump of brush at high speed. He will be completely out of sight in the time it takes you to blink.

More times than not, when a whitetail approaches a fence, he stops and studies it, walks up and down to choose his crossing spot, and finally comes over. This particular buck was apparently more decisive than most, because he came trotting across the open pasture and went directly over as though he knew exactly where he was going.

In my pursuit of whitetails I try many different approaches in order to get the shots that I do. Among other things I always try to "be ready" when I'm in whitetail country. You just never know what the next turn may bring. I took the larger photograph above from the driver's side window of my truck as I jerked to a halt in a small clearing in the midst of some very heavy timber. He may look calm, but he wasn't there but an instant. I looked for him the rest of the year, but never found him. Early the next fall I was rattling antlers in the same general area and lo and behold, look who just arrived in the smaller photo. I only saw him these two times and once again at a great distance. Such is the nature of many of my efforts.

DANCING WITH DEER

It is one thing to SEE a whitetail buck out in the woods or pasture. It is quite another matter entirely to get yourself in a position to come up with nice, attractive photographs of those same bucks which are so (relatively) easy to SEE. When people see shots such as the early morning situation above, they tend to imagine that it was luck or happenstance. More times than not, these shots come only after much teeth-gnashing, several close-but-no-cigar failures, and no small amount of figuring and conniving. When they do finally present themselves (if ever), the window of opportunity is usually extremely brief.

Learning as quickly as they do in their evolutionary process, whitetails have easily figured out a myriad of ways to avoid my presence. Sometimes it seems as if whitetails, *as a species*, have learned to outwit me, as though that specific ability to beat me personally were inborn in each individual. They have given me the slip in every way imaginable. Granted, I win a small battle once in a while, but overall, whitetails are easily winning the war.

I work hard at trying to get close to whitetails for a variety of reasons ... as a hunter, as a whitetail photographer, as a naturalist and simply as a person who thoroughly enjoys their existence. While tactics and techniques may vary according to the specific hunting mode, there are common threads that run through all of

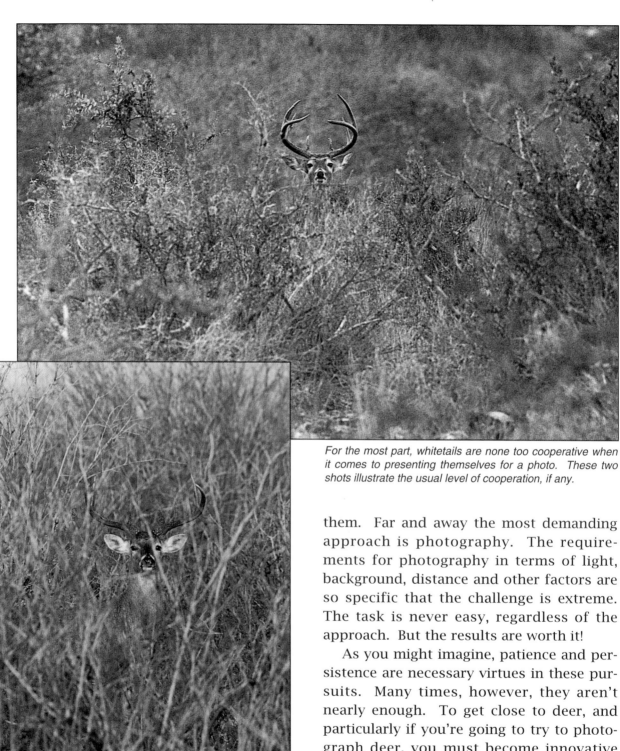

For the most part, whitetails are none too cooperative when it comes to presenting themselves for a photo. These two shots illustrate the usual level of cooperation, if any.

them. Far and away the most demanding approach is photography. The requirements for photography in terms of light, background, distance and other factors are so specific that the challenge is extreme. The task is never easy, regardless of the approach. But the results are worth it!

As you might imagine, patience and persistence are necessary virtues in these pursuits. Many times, however, they aren't nearly enough. To get close to deer, and particularly if you're going to try to photograph deer, you must become innovative and open-minded in your thinking. There are two well-known precepts that must become an integral part of your thinking. ... *Never say die!* and *Anything is possible!* With whitetails anything *is* possible.

Spending as much time among deer as I do, I've had a wide variety of whitetail experiences. In the beginning I mostly sat in traditional deer stands and just waited. I saw many deer that way and came back with quite a few photographs. However, in time, I began to go after whitetails a little more aggressively, defining and testing the limits as I went. I've tried many different things in my dances with deer as I struggled to figure out ways to outwit them ... scents, camouflages, all kinds of blinds, sitting, standing, laying, rattling, calling, grunting, on the ground, in the air, walking, running, driving, and all sorts of individual touches depending on the situation. Some worked, and some didn't.

One of the things I've tried that produced some of the most remarkable results has been the extremely basic idea of just following deer through the woods. Before you start snickering, let me tell you a little more. I know it sounds unlikely that I would be able to follow a wild deer through the woods. Most of the time that's true, but not always. On the occasions when it does work, the results are so remarkable that each success is worth the risk of several failures.

The secret to following deer successfully, and at close range, is in your initial approach and in your postures and attitudes. Your initial approach (meaning that point at which you first make yourself visible to the deer) must be quiet and innocuous. It is a matter of providing full disclosure of your presence with no predatory signals whatsoever.

This is a really big whitetail buck climbing an extremely steep hill. He went up several hundred yards of this kind of incline, and much of it was a lot rougher than this with thick brush and huge boulders. After he disappeared, I followed and found that the trail led to a small, high, remote, almost impenetrable sanctuary. I've learned that many of the more mature bucks bed in such places, and I try to seek out this type of difficult and remote terrain.

If you think that it didn't take some serious dancing, and planning, and trying, and hoping, to get this photo ....think again! This is not a "manufactured" or sandwiched moon-shot like most of those you see. It's the real thing — a real deer, with a real moon rising over him, on Kodachrome. The exact combination of conditions that create the "potential" for this shot occur only a few times each year!

Any attempt whatever to sneak or hide will be taken as a predatory posture. Incidentally, you'd want to do this at some distance. There's no distance rule, but if you step out in front of a deer at very close range, it's an almost guaranteed failure. You'll lose most of the deer during the initial approach, anyway. However, if you're careful with the presentation, there will be a few deer now and then that will not run away at the initial disclosure. This does not mean that you're home free. This strictly "nonpredatory" posture must be maintained at all times. It's important that the deer begins to perceive you as just another animal in the woods, calm and nonthreatening. Try to avoid looking at the deer directly, particularly avoiding eye contact. Convey a sense of nonchalance, if possible. I prefer to walk in random directions (generally paralleling the deer), and I intentionally make a bit of noise to help him be fully aware of my location. The use of scent or camouflage is of little or no value since there is no hiding.

With caution and patience, it's sometimes possible to gradually work closer to the deer, keeping in mind that he could be lost at any point. A good understanding of whitetail body language is essential. Close attention must be paid to his every move in order to be aware of his alarm status. It's important to know when to back off and give him more space. I use these clues to tell me when I might or might not be able to take a photo.

I've now had a considerable number of different experiences "following" deer. In my book, "*Amazing Whitetails*," I chronicled the remarkable events that took place as I followed one particularly interesting buck for over five hours, non-stop. There have been several others that I've stayed with for hours at a time, and many more that I've followed anywhere from just a few minutes to perhaps half an hour. They're all very individual animals and each responds to this type of intrusion a little differently. Further, I've found that a deer that will be tolerant on one occasion will

The pursuit of whitetails frequently produces outcomes which are not quite what you had in mind. I had gone to a great deal of effort and discomfort to be in a certain blind for several fruitless mornings in a row when finally, on a foggy morning, I took this photo. I had seen this buck before, but had never been able to get close. I took the foggy shot just as it was barely light enough to do so. It was my LAST shot, because two ranch hands came roaring over the hill in a pickup, and he ran away for good. Disruptions such as this seem to happen all too frequently.

The buck above really got my goat. He was a wild buck, but was seen around the ranch pretty frequently. I had been there for several days and had spent a good deal of time trying to see or locate this buck — with absolutely no success. I had just about given up on the idea of seeing him at all. Then, of all things, I was at the ranch headquarters about noon when I happened to glance beyond the barns to a junkyard area. Near it was a large grain silo where corn was stored (and frequently spilled). And who should be standing there in broad daylight in the middle of the day? Naturally, when I tried to slip around the barn, he disappeared back into the heavy brush.

not necessarily be tolerant on a different day. In fact, I treat each such success as a once-in-a-lifetime event. There have only been two or three times when I was able to have a repeat success with the same deer.

When it does work, "following" deer can give you insights into the private lives of deer in their own environment that you would probably never observe otherwise. It's like being inside the bowl *with* the goldfish. You may gain some entirely different perspectives on the whitetail world.

One thing I've learned, watching whitetails over the years, is to always expect the unexpected. This predictable unpredictability is part of their charm, even if it

The picture above has quite a story behind it. This buck had come running to my rattling horns earlier in the day. When he saw me and walked away, I decided to follow him. I sauntered around in the woods at a distance from him until he finally accepted me, more or less, and I followed him with a camera for about five hours. During this time a number of events occurred, but one in particular led to the above photo. We crossed many small creeks in the woods over several hours. It was standard for him to walk up to the edge, look at the bottom and the other side, and then take one bound to the bottom and one more up the other bank. As he approached yet another small creek, he looked and leapt as usual, except that he accidentally caught one hind leg in a vine on the bank and went head over heels into a pool of water. He came out like a bullet and then seemed to look around to see if anyone had seen the embarrassing incident. He was soaked and spent several minutes trying to shake off the water. You just don't expect things like that to happen to a graceful whitetail, but once in a while they happen.

This is a terrific buck. I spent several days in this location, but saw him only once, just at dark. Unfortunately, there have been many such bucks which I've seen only once, and never again.

does confuse and frustrate humans to no end. It often seems to exist primarily for that purpose. Unpredictability is one of the qualities that makes them so challenging and so intriguing.

The more you watch deer, the more unusual things you'll see. For example, I watched the buck at the top of page 72 as he tripped and fell head over heels into a creek full of water. That was unexpected!

I once watched a truly antlerless buck actually breeding a doe. *He didn't even have pedicels on his head*, but I could clearly see his genitals as he bred the doe!

Another wild buck that I was observing mounted a doe decoy repeatedly, finally knocking it over. It was especially unusual because the buck had already dropped his antlers. Then, to top it off, two buzzards flew down to check out the "dead" decoy.

I've seen coyotes chasing deer and deer chasing coyotes. Deer have interacted with a variety of other animals as I watched. All manner of incredible fighting and other behavior have been presented, mostly when it was too dark to take photos. I've even

With the attitude that you never know for sure until you try, I've learned that sometimes it is possible to follow a wild whitetail in his own environment, and in plain sight. Most times it doesn't work, but when it does it offers some great educational insights as well as some unique photo opportunities. I've followed some deer for only 30 seconds, but I've followed several others for hours at a time. I was successful with both of the bucks on this page. It's a unique experience when it works.

At times whitetails can be amazingly curious. Once in a while, sometimes quite carelessly, a deer will approach a blind, a truck, or even an unhidden photographer, and check it out. Of course this is in direct and flagrant violation of all the usual whitetail rules of safety and general behavior. It doesn't happen too often, but it's the best way to get a butterfly eye's view of a deer.

been viciously attacked — by a doe! The very same doe you see on the facing page, standing demurely in my truck, became very tame and gentle over the years, even though she ranged out on the ranch. Some six or seven years after the incident when she got into my truck, I was driving through a pasture about daybreak when I saw her and three other deer. She was acting very dominant toward the other deer, one of which was a handsome young buck. The other deer were not approachable, but I thought that if I put out some feed and backed off that they might become more at ease. When I got out of the truck to carry a bucket-lid full of feed to the field, the tame doe became indignant that I wouldn't give her the feed then and there. She reared up on her hind legs and began kicking the living daylights out of me, flailing at me with her front hooves. I was fortunate that most of her blows hit my chest and arms rather than my face. I was taken completely by surprise. It only proved the well-known fact that you must never trust *any* whitetail at close range, especially if they have become gentle or tame.

I've had some great experiences getting close to deer by using camouflage and the knowledge of their poor depth perception. Last year I scouted and found a remote area to hunt that had a massive scrape line down an open path that led to a cross-fence. The next day, I was fully camouflaged, and I took a long, circuitous route to the location so that I wouldn't spook deer as I walked in. I sat on the bare ground under the branches of a

I was sitting in a blind near a waterhole when this buck came over a fence. He seemed familiar to me, but I couldn't place him. He faded back into the brush, only to reappear later. He still looked familiar. When I looked very closely, I noticed the small notch on his left brow-tine and the bit of roughness at the base of his left tall tine. I realized that he was a buck that I'd seen only once, about a mile away and two months previously. He had broken off the second and fourth tines on his left side, changing his appearance.

small bush on the fenceline, and waited. Thirty minutes before sundown, a mature seven-point buck came down a visible trail that was parallel to the fence. As I sat frozen in place, he dawdled around and browsed only four or five yards from me. As he took another step, I realized that the deer trail went exactly past my knee, and that he might accidentally touch me in three or four more steps. He had fresh wounds on his neck and a freshly broken tine from fighting. I had visions of his being startled by my smell at a range of only a foot or two, and perhaps striking out, hooking me with his antlers. I was in a remote spot over a half mile from the nearest dirt road. As he reached a range of four feet, I gently raised one hand a few inches, and he went ballistic. This was pretty exciting stuff, considering that there was nothing between us but thin air, and

This doe had become gentle and somewhat fearless, and I occasionally stopped and fed her. Once, when I got out of the truck and turned my back, she was instantly inside, looking for corn!

Rattling for bucks can produce just about as many different types of scenarios as anything. You just never know what's going to happen. Sometimes the bucks come in right on top of you, as with the buck at the upper left. I rattled him up in heavy brush in Mexico. At times it's one quick shot at a distance, such as the upper right. Occasionally, you rattle up a doe instead of a buck.

Only about eight feet separates the spots where these two bucks jumped the fence, but the buck on the right made his jump approximately 15 or 20 minutes before the other buck came over. If you look closely, you'll see that the quality of the light is a little different in the two photos. Anytime I'm lucky enough to see two jumps like this in one afternoon, it was a good day.

further, that I was sitting on the ground looking *up* at a 200 pound rutting buck.

I've also had great experiences "rattling up" deer. There is no more exciting way in the world to go after whitetails than rattling antlers. I've rattled up young bucks, middle-aged bucks and old, mature bucks — bucks of all sizes and descriptions. I rattle loudly and aggressively and the results have been phenomenal. I don't keep count anymore, but I've certainly rattled up over a thousand bucks and a surprising number of does. Sometimes there's a big buck behind the doe.

A while back, I set up to rattle in the middle of a large area of heavy brush. I was on the ground and there was a small clearing in front of me. As I first rattled and kicked brush, I could see color coming my way through the brush. The mature buck stopped at the edge of the clearing and stared directly at me without seeing through the camouflage. His right antler was behind an overhanging limb. The visible, left antler had seven points. I wanted to verify the antlers before I shot, but he whirled and left without revealing them. I rattled him back *six times*, and he hid the antler each time until the last. Then, another mature buck also came, and the first buck moved over to reveal a broken main beam. What an exciting afternoon!

You can see by the faces and body sizes that the buck on the right is an older, more mature deer. The buck on the left is a middle-aged deer with a lot of "attitude." He is the one who actually approached the older deer and initiated this kick-boxing free-for-all. In the end the older deer knocked the other buck down and ran him away. The small yearling buck with the front-row seat is getting an eye full. In a few years he very likely will be as rambunctious as the buck on the left and might very well be challenging him at that time.

≡ LORDS OF THE MEADOWS ≡

In most social structures there are a few individuals who would be king. In the whitetail kingdom, EVERYBODY wants to be king. The natural dominance structuring of whitetail society demands that each individual aspire to be at the top of the hierarchy. Consequently, every time two whitetails meet, one will try to lord it over the other. The stronger, more experienced bucks will make their way to the top.

Whitetails may appear to be some of the most peaceful, gentle animals in the woods, but don't believe it for a minute, at least not where their social behavior is concerned. They just tend to keep their aggressive demeanor out of sight until it's called for. It always lurks there, just beneath the surface, and it can be called out of retirement in a flash!

It's a good thing that whitetails don't have big teeth, long claws or some of the other weaponry usually associated with dangerous animals. If they did, they'd probably kill each other so often that their entire species would soon expire. They're bad enough with antlers and hooves.

Believe it or not, there's a good reason for all this meanness. It's part of the basic social behavior that creates structure in whitetail society. It is primarily through dominance posturing and aggression that the hierarchy, or pecking order, is formed and maintained. Overall, it's very beneficial

Dominance posturing takes place throughout the year. The two bucks at the top have dropped their antlers, yet the process goes on. In the third photo, an older, more dominant buck backs down a huge, but younger and more timid buck. In the bottom shot, the same huge, timid buck has turned around and backed down another buck which has bigger antlers than the one he just backed away from.

to the species, even though some individuals are injured or even killed along the way. This may sound rather harsh, but the constant battle to be "king of the hill" keeps the weaker bloodlines from being perpetuated throughout the herd. A major factor in the overall success of whitetails, as a species, has been their selective, "survival of the fittest" process. The strongest, most aggressive bucks ultimately rule the pecking order and do most of the breeding. Their stronger, more aggressive characteristics are passed on to their offspring, and the results are compounded with each additional generation.

The aggressive tendencies of whitetails are at least partially instinctive. Young fawns begin posturing toward each other almost as soon as they're up and around. There's no doubt that some of this behavior is also learned. The young bucks very quickly get a strong taste of the negative side of it as they try to mingle with the older deer. At times the older bucks are quite tolerant of the extremely young deer, but at times they are not.

One interesting thing that I see very frequently is a situation where a mature buck (or one that is relatively mature) seems to be accompanied by a younger buck as though the younger deer is his "sidekick." My friend, Dr. James Kroll, calls the younger buck in this situation a "toady." It's almost as though the younger buck is traveling as an apprentice to the older deer, learning the tricks of the trade along the way.

The "dominance factor," which is the driving force behind all these aggressive tendencies, is a constant, 365-days-a-year presence. Aggression among whitetail bucks increases with the advent of the rut, but the basic process goes on all year long. Even in the spring when the exhausted, rut-weary bucks have dropped their antlers, and during the early summer months when life in whitetail land seems so peaceful, there continues to be a constant day-to-day struggle for dominance. On any given day of the year, this competition is just as natural and ordinary for a deer as waking up in the morning.

Whitetail bucks are quick to use their hooves during the times when they are growing new velvet antlers. Some of the flailing is just a matter of posturing more aggressively, but it doesn't take much encouragement for the posturing to turn into a full fledged, knock-down-drag-out, kick-boxing match. The hooves are sharp and the bucks frequently aim for the face, neck and antlers.

The dominant buck at the upper left became so incensed when the other buck didn't defer to his posturing that he literally knocked him flat on the ground. I suspect that his posturing was more effective thereafter. At the upper right, the smaller buck is exhibiting a submissive posture by crouching and stretching his neck and chin out. In the photo at the middle right, both bucks appear to be very mature. Dominance behavior persists throughout a whitetail's life. The buck at the bottom left makes a particularly imposing figure.

Whitetail dominance behavior is not reserved only for the bucks. Female deer certainly put in their fair share of posturing and kick-boxing, among themselves as well as with the bucks. It is not at all unusual to see a mature whitetail doe that is dominant over certain bucks, particularly bucks which are very young, very old, sick, or just timid. Does are heavily involved in the kick-boxing behavior all year round, whereas the bucks tend to use this tactic only when they have velvet antlers or no antlers.

As the days begin to shorten, and the velvet is removed, bucks begin to get more and more edgy as their testosterone level increases. They become obsessive about dominance. The buck at the left is thrashing the brush to impress another nearby deer.

The struggle for dominance, as a year-round phenomenon, is one of the most interesting aspects of whitetail behavior to be studied. Whitetail bucks are masters in "the art of the threat," and there are many different mannerisms and postures which are used. It's amazing how much communication can be achieved with such seemingly minor nuances of posture. By tweaking the nuances ever so slightly, the levels of seriousness can be elevated or lowered.

Far and away, the most commonly used threat posture is the "hard stare," which is nothing more than just that. Direct eye contact, and especially prolonged direct eye contact, serves as the whitetail equivalent of, "I don't want you to come any closer, and if you do, we may have to fight!"

Beyond the hard stare, there is a whole series of other nuances which will take buck-to-buck communication to all kinds of different levels. Ear positions, neck positions, the rolling of the eyes, the bowing of the back, the angle of antler presentation, the turn of the head, the angle of the chin, the sneer of a "snort-wheeze," the hair standing up on the neck, the pawing of the ground, even the "busting" of brush in intimidation threats ... all these things mean something important to any whitetail buck which is watching. And they're *all* watching. Bucks are very attentive to all possible signals.

There are many different nuances which whitetail bucks use in posturing and threatening each other. The buck at the top is vigorously pawing the ground and kicking up dirt as he threatens another buck. The photo at the bottom is a classic view of the "hard stare." The hard stare is perhaps the most used and most effective visual communication behavior utilized by whitetails as they continually practice "the art of the threat." The buck on the right is warning the other deer NOT to come any closer.

Some threats are obviously more serious than others, particularly if the two bucks are fairly evenly matched. You can tell at a glance that both situations on this page are quite serious. The two bucks at the top had a short but serious fight. In the photo at the left, both bucks held absolutely rigid in this super-close position for a long time, perhaps 10 seconds or more. Then they cautiously backed away from each other.

There's one major difference in the nature of the whitetail aggression that takes place in the spring and summer months, as opposed to the fall and winter months. In the spring, when the bucks have no antlers, and during the summer, when they have velvet antlers, they don't use their heads or antlers for fighting. During these periods they still carry out all the traditional posturing, but when it comes down to a fight, it's going to be a kick-boxing match with their hooves. These bouts may look "cute," like they're dancing, but they are as serious as can be. The hooves are sharp, their legs are extremely quick and powerful, and they frequently aim for the face or tender velvet antlers, sometimes drawing blood. Occasionally, one will actually knock the other out cold.

In the fall and winter, much of the basic posturing is the same, but when it's time to fight, antlers are now the weapon of choice. When a buck removes his velvet, he will immediately begin fighting with his antlers instead of his hooves. Of course the antlers are potentially more devastating than hooves, and a considerable number of bucks are seriously injured or killed each year. No matter what time of

In the fall whitetail bucks do a lot of head-cocking and side-stepping as they push each other around. It's the constant reinforcement of dominance, the constant reminder that one or the other is "the boss." In the top photo, the buck on the right is dominant even though the other has much larger antlers. The small, dominant buck pushed the big non-typical out of sight. In the bottom photo, one buck was bedded down, minding his own business, when the other buck walked stiffly over to him and began hooking his antlers.

Usually, when there is an altercation between two bucks, it is carried out in the form of a "sparring match." Most of these pushing matches aren't all that serious, but they're still exciting to see. These "tests" help the bucks to build up their confidence levels as they get a feel for the necessary moves. They are in effect practice sessions in preparation for the real battles yet to come. The majority of bucks that are involved in sparring matches are young and middle-aged deer, but as always there are exceptions.

The photos on this page are excerpts from serious, knock-down-drag-out fights. Once the rut has arrived, each buck seems to walk around with an imaginary line drawn at the limits of what he considers to be his own personal space. Once the line is crossed by another buck, a fight is inevitable. When the bucks are evenly matched, both in terms of body size as well as "attitude," the fights can be utterly vicious. It is quite literally a life-or-death situation as they single-mindedly try to kill each other.

This is a very old buck, nine or ten years old. I'd seen him before and he had always been a very dominant buck. As you can see, he has now lost an eye in one of his many battles.

Bucks pay little attention to injuries during the rut. This buck has an oozing gash on his neck, but he's so involved with the season that he's lip-curling and going about his business.

Here's an old warrior if I ever saw one. He appears to be very mature, and there's a big chunk of hide ripped off the back of his neck. He exhibited a considerable "attitude."

This buck acted as though he didn't feel very well, and it's easy to see why. He'd been fighting and his bottom lip was ripped loose, the back of his head was bloody, and he was limping.

Whitetails are NOT benevolent animals at all when it comes to their own sick, old or injured. In the photo at the upper left, the older buck has lost a foot, and the yearling buck is pushing him around. The upper right photo shows a large-bodied, healthy buck posturing to a very sickly-looking, runty, little buck. He pushed him around unmercifully. The bottom photo shows a yearling buck who was dogging an ancient buck relentlessly. When a whitetail buck gets down and out, he is severely persecuted by the other deer.

year they're fighting, the winner likely will be the buck with the heaviest body weight or the buck with the most aggressive attitude. In the majority of battles, I would tend to favor the buck with the attitude. There are certainly other factors such as age and experience, but body size and attitude will always weigh heavily.

If you will observe and study all the various nuances of posture associated with the whitetail dominance factor, it will greatly enhance your enjoyment of the time spent among deer. You'll find tremendous satisfaction in your ability to understand and predict their actions and reactions. Your time in the woods will no longer be spent *just looking at deer* — rather it will become a front row seat to an ages-old social process full of drama and suspense. If you're lucky, that front row seat may drop an experience of a lifetime right in your lap as you watch two fearless adversaries go for the crown.

One of the great things about spending a lot of time with whitetails is that over time you're likely to see any number of deer with unique qualities. Further, from time to time you will see situations and behaviors which are equally unique. It's very unusual to see three big bucks this close to each other once the rut has been initiated. Usually, mature bucks keep well away from each other during this period. The three bucks above are practically in formation. Also, the two bucks in the back are nearly identical, possibly due to genetics.

The bachelor groups of summer offer some of the most exciting and interesting situations for whitetail enthusiasts. At no other time of the year will you find bucks to be as concentrated or as visually accessible. By seeing a large number of bucks in close proximity, you can more easily key in on those behavioral and physical attributes which are normal, and those which are not.

Wow, look at that! Good grief! That's incredible! Unbelievable! I've *never* seen anything like that before! Common everyday phrases of exclamation such as these and others really get a workout in whitetail land. The whitetail universe is absolutely *filled* with quirks, oddities, aberrations and extreme or unusual situations of all kinds. If you spend enough time in the woods, there's just no telling what you'll eventually see. One of the greatest things about going into the deer woods is that every time you go, it's

with the realization that all sorts of interesting situations are possible. There's a lot to be discovered out there!

I've seen and experienced things that I would never have imagined — three-legged deer, white deer, black deer, unicorn deer, stag bucks, antlered does, maned deer, freak deer and all kinds of weird stuff. The possibility of finding these types of unusual things really adds spice to the whitetail experience. And it's not that normal whitetails are boring. That's not the case at all. These oddities simply expand the possibilities in a world that is already very exciting.

This is a **"piebald"** doe. That is the word generally used to describe deer that are partially white. Some may have only a few white patches, while others are almost totally white. These deer are not the same as albino deer. The eyes, nose and parts of the body are normal color, unlike a true albino.

There is a tremendous range of color values within the normal coloration parameters of whitetails. This buck is so dark that he is essentially black. Often you will find very dark and very light individuals within the same local area.

The unusual things that you see while watching deer aren't necessarily just physical oddities of the deer themselves. Some of the most interesting sightings have to do with strange, bizarre or unusual deer *behavior*. Some of the behavior may not be all that rare, but it can still be quite entertaining to watch, especially if you haven't seen it before. There's a wide assortment of odd behaviors to be observed. For instance, have you ever watched as one deer frantically chased another in high-speed circles? This behavior is particularly noticeable among does, fawns and young bucks at gathering spots such as waterholes. Typically, a group of deer will have gathered at one of these places, when suddenly, such a chase will begin. Frequently, much of the running is done in the edge of the water, and there is a lot of noise and

This has to be one of the most unusual whitetail bucks ever photographed. Is he weird — or what? I saw this buck only one time, briefly, as he stuck his head from behind the cedar bush and then high-tailed it across a small opening. Incredibly, the property owner had found the shed antler(s) from this buck the previous year and they were similar but a little smaller. Both antlers sprout from one single pedicel which practically covers his entire head and part of his face. The buck's face is grotesquely malformed, with bizarre, oversized eyeballs which are displaced and bugged-out by the massive amount of bone. He's unbelievable.

And you thought whitetails didn't have a sense of humor! I could almost swear that these bucks look like some people I've seen. For all the world, they appear to be grinning or smiling. In both cases they were chasing does when I caught them in the open. Maybe they had good reason to be smiling. More likely, they were winded and hot from so much chasing and were trying to catch their breath.

splashing. Then, as suddenly as it began, the chase will end. These don't seem to be dominance displays at all. About the only explanation I have, after watching many of these chases, is that it is done for the pure, unadulterated joy and fun of it!

Another (unrelated) behavior that I've been privileged to witness several times has to do with multiple bucks chasing a doe that is in estrus. Most of the time I'm lucky if I see *one* buck chasing a doe.

However, in circumstances where there is a relatively large buck population and/or a fairly even buck-to-doe ratio, it's not all that uncommon to see several bucks chasing after one doe. All that competition creates some extremely interesting social interaction. It's really something to see when a doe is leading a small army of would-be suitors around by the nose. I've seen as many as six, seven or even eight different bucks that were all after the same doe at the same time. It's weird enough if they're just standing around, as in a food plot or field. That situation calls for all kinds of posturing and sidling, with the biggest buck trying to ward off the approaches of all the lesser bucks. But just wait until she decides to run, and I mean really **run**, perhaps through thick brush or woods, with seven or eight bucks in hot pursuit. In most cases the wild chase quickly organizes into a single-file lineup, like a high-speed snake dance winding through the woods. Soon after the frantic chase begins, the most dominant buck will have worked his way into the first position behind the doe. The second most dominant buck will be in the second position, the third buck in the pecking order will be

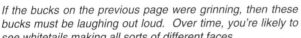

If the bucks on the previous page were grinning, then these bucks must be laughing out loud. Over time, you're likely to see whitetails making all sorts of different faces.

third, and so on down the line. All this order and structure is quite well maintained, even though all the animals are running full-out at top speed! If one buck gets too close to the one in front of him, the leading buck will whirl and push him out of line. The spacing varies somewhat, but generally it's as tight as the leading bucks will allow the following bucks to be. The entire event is really quite a circus when there are so many bucks involved. It's almost like a Keystone Kops routine if the doe or the leading buck should stop suddenly. I've seen that happen a couple of times, and the result was much like a chain-reaction automobile accident on a

There are a number of unusual physical characteristics that whitetails may exhibit, such as the distinctly translucent, amber eyes on all four of the bucks on these two pages.

freeway. There were bucks flying every which way as they came around a bush or over a hill and almost piled into each other, unexpectedly. It was wild!

Another strange behavior that I've witnessed multiple times involves only one deer, either buck or doe, that began to make high, twisting, standing jumps in a tight circle. There seemed to be some indication of an extreme frustration such as an unscratchable itch, or perhaps a bug deep in a nose or ear. I've watched deer perform this awkward dance for long periods of time, as much as 10 or 15 minutes at a stretch. Then, as though it never happened, they calmly went on their way.

Deer with amber eyes are quite scarce. I've seen perhaps eight or nine bucks that had them. Oddly, I have never seen, or at least never noticed, amber eyes on a doe.

The two photos at the top of the page illustrate the vast differences that exist from one animal to another in terms of neck and body size. Both bucks were photographed in Texas. The buck on the left is slightly older and was photographed a little later in the year, but the disparity is still very notable. The differences are related more to individuality than to age. The pictures at the bottom of the page illustrate another kind of comparison, using a different deer. Both pictures show the same buck, photographed at the left in late September and at the right in late November of the same year. The muscle tone and neck size of a whitetail buck can make a remarkable transformation as he prepares for the rut.

Here are some more examples of whitetail necks. The buck above is muscled up as though he has been working out in a gym. The buck on the right looks like there was a giraffe in his gene pool. When deer get very tense and alarmed as he is, they can really stretch their necks out in order to get better visibility.

Some of the most exciting behavior that I've watched has been in association with the rut, especially the knock-down, drag-out fights that I've been lucky enough to see. As the peak of the rut approaches, the really mature, truly dominant bucks are something to behold. They've got surrealistic necks and attitudes to match. They get so wound up about defending their "personal space" and other dominance activities that they begin to look and act like overgrown school-yard bullies. Obviously, some of the most interesting, interactive behavior takes place during this period. Usually there is a single buck who is "lord and master" of an immediate area. Frequently he is very obnoxious, much like some people you've known. I've seen large, super-dominant bucks like this take a well-attended waterhole or feeding area as their

Here are some rut-related behaviors that you may not have seen. The top photo shows a buck following a doe trail across an oat patch with his nose. The arch of his back and position of his tail indicate that he is aroused by the odors. The middle picture shows a buck traveling at midday with his mouth hanging open. He's probably been following doe scent trails for hours or even days, and he's hot and winded from the relentless chase. The big buck at the bottom of the page is performing autoerotic sexual behavior. During the rut bucks occasionally get frustrated and/or excited and perform without a partner.

own personal property, not allowing any other bucks to get within 50 yards of the water, food or any does which may be present. He may act as though he's eating or drinking, but every time any other buck crosses some imaginary line that he's drawn in the sand, his hair stands on end as he starts sidling toward his next victim. There's a tremendous amount of showmanship involved in these displays, and it's quite rare for any of the peripheral bucks to take him on. There's no way. He's just *too bad!*

Then, once in a great while, I've been allowed to sit in awe of that most dramatic of all whitetail behaviors, a truly serious fight between two fully mature bucks. There's nothing else like it in the world. Occasionally, when one of those super-dominant bucks has assumed control of what he considers to be *his* domain, another buck appears, perhaps a "dominant floater" traveling far beyond his normal range looking for does in estrus. If the intruder happens to be mature and aggressive, this creates an explosive situation, the kind most likely to escalate into a full-blown war. The bucks aren't familiar with each other so they don't have an established pecking order between them, and without order there is chaos. Beyond that, the testosterone is boiling in their systems like hot oil, and they are on such an edge that they're highly intolerant of *anything* that doesn't please them. Unless one of them grossly out-classes the other, there's going to be one heck of a fight.

The stamina and brute strength exhibited during these fights is nothing less than supernatural. Can you even imagine the power it takes to push a struggling, two hundred pound adversary backwards, through dense brush, breaking off wrist-sized limbs as they go? How much strength do you suppose it takes to pick up and flip that same, opposing two hundred pounds, mainly by using neck and shoulder muscles? The adrenaline flow must be incredible. These kinds of battles can quickly get out of hand, because there are absolutely no rules. The bucks get so mad, so agitated, that you can practically feel their hatred. The goal is always to force the opponent into total submission, but frequently the attitudes are "kill, or be killed!" These kinds of fights are not observed very often by people, but when they are, it's a memory of a lifetime. I've seen far more than my share, at least thirty serious fights, but keep in mind that I've also spent literally thousands of hours in the field watching deer.

The bucks in the two photos above are grooming each other. This is a social behavior which is seen from time to time, usually during the pre-rut and post-rut periods. Even though it appears to be a mutual "friendly" gesture, it seems to be related to, and perhaps a part of, the overall dominance behavior of whitetails. Scents tasted and smelled may help reinforce the pecking order.

This bizarre looking little buck has somewhat of a problem. I have seen variations of this type of antler deformity on yearling bucks enough times now that it almost seems that this is a problem peculiar to this age-class. At first glance it would seem that the antler is flopping and loose, but in fact it is solid and firm in its position. This particular buck even rubbed a tree with it.

This is an example of a common minor antler deformity caused during the growth sequence. The crooked point was hit and bent during the velvet period and hardened in that position.

The more time you spend "up close and personal" with deer, the more unusual things you will eventually see. Many of these interesting things will be obvious to you at a glance. Other things will require a little closer attention on your part if you are to fully appreciate everything that whitetails have to offer. Many times it takes a bit of detective work to understand the nature of some of the strange things seen in the deer woods. Some thoughtful reasoning and logical deduction are frequently required. For instance, if you were to see a deer with velvet antlers during the month of December, would you instantly know what you were looking at? Possibly not. There would be a chance that the velvet-antlered deer might be a doe, or it could be a buck with a hormonal problem. It could even be a buck that has somehow lost his genitals, either to injury or disease. Any of these things, and possibly more,

This is a **doe**! The previous year she had four-point velvet antlers, but the soft antlers froze during the winter and the beams broke off below the forks. I saw her for three years and as far as I know these stubby antlers were never shed.

This buck has no testicles, and his velvet antlers are permanent. Last year's antlers froze, broke off, and started regrowing again.

This photo, taken in early August, shows an extremely rare buck. These are his **undropped,** hardened antlers carried over from the previous year!

This also is very rare. At first glance it appears that this buck has shed one antler. However, if you'll look closely, you'll see that he does not have an antler pedicel on his left side. He will **never** have more than one antler.

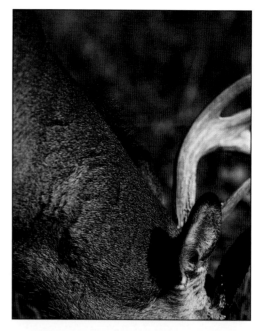

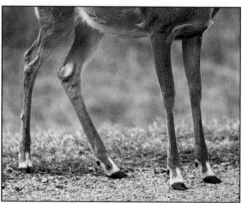

The buck at the above left has lost his tail and only has a tiny stub left. I don't know how he did it, but he is the third buck I've seen with no tail. The buck at the upper right has a distinct mane. The fawn at the lower right has white feet, sort of like the "socks" that cats and dogs sometimes have. I've seen quite a few different deer in different places with white feet such as these.

could be the cause of such an unusual sight. There are many other examples of situations that require some thought.

You might see a buck that has only one antler. Depending on the time of year, that could mean he has already shed one antler. A bloody pedicel observed in late winter or early spring would indicate that's probably the case. The same sight in September or October might indicate that the missing antler has been ripped out from the pedicel in a fight. I've seen that. It might even turn out, when you looked more closely, that there is the remaining stub of a beam,

broken off in a fight. At a distance, or in low light, it might not have been obvious. There are still other possibilities. It could be a rare situation such as the one shown at the bottom right on page 105, where the buck has only one pedicel and will always be one-antlered during the fall seasons. You just won't know these things until you look at the situation closely.

What would you think if you saw two big bucks at a distance, right in each other's face, with their heads vigorously bobbing up and down? Closer examination might reveal that it was two bucks performing mutual grooming behavior, each licking the other's face and neck. This is a social behavior that is usually seen during the pre-rut and post-rut periods. Even though it may appear to be something of a friendly gesture, it seems to be related to, and perhaps a part of, dominance behavior. I once watched two large bucks performing this behavior so fervently that they were almost pushing each other over. It became so dramatic and forceful that I felt sure it would escalate into a fight, but it didn't.

Many of the small but interesting aberrations of deer will be missed entirely unless you are quite observant. It's very easy *not* to notice that a deer might be missing a tail, or have a scar on his face or perhaps have amber-colored eyes like the bucks on pages 98 and 99. It would be very easy to miss the fact that a buck had a small mane, a black tail or maybe "white stocking" feet.

Here's a one-of-a-kind buck. He has suffered a BROKEN NECK, yet survived it. His neck has fused into a permanent left-hand turn. Even when he is looking forward or running, he always has that stiff, sharp left turn in his neck.

This is a severe and life-threatening injury. Somehow, perhaps in a fight, this buck has severely broken his bottom jaw to the extent that he can't even close his mouth. That's why you see him here drinking from the pond with his entire nose completely submerged. Otherwise he wouldn't be able to create any suction to get water. Usually when a buck suffers a severe, disfiguring injury such as this, the other bucks will try to dominate him and will not tolerate his presence. This buck, however, was still acting quite dominant.

There's a great deal of relativity to be observed in watching whitetails. For instance, just look at the size difference between the fawn and the mature buck at the top of the page. You might not realize that one is so small or the other so large if they weren't standing side by side. At the bottom of the page, this buck looks quite different in late September (left photo) than he does in late November (right photo).

When you get up close and personal with deer, you begin to see all kinds of interesting scenes. At the top left, the buck is trying to shake a bug out of his ear. The top right photo shows a nice young buck with a breakfast partner. The unusual photo just above shows two bucks watching the approach of another.

If you will be truly observant and carefully study the deer that you see, you'll find that there is very often more than meets the eye, or at least more than meets the casual eye. Those people who go into the woods and see only "ordinary" deer are probably not taking in all there is to see, and they're missing plenty in the process. There's a lot of great stuff out there.

To be "up close and personal" with whitetails is to be intimate with their quirks and peculiarities. It allows you to see unique things that many people will never experience, and the more you see, the more intrigued you'll become. All this will make you more knowledgeable about whitetails in general. It's the kind of knowledge that will not only give you great personal satisfaction, but will also help you in your future pursuit and understanding of deer, whether you are a hunter, photographer or any other kind of whitetail "nut."

Would you have recognized this buck from one year to the next? If you pay close attention to the details of a deer's appearance, it is quite easy to recognize individuals from year to year. In the upper right photo he was 2½ years old. In the upper left shot he was 3½ years old, and in the large picture he was 4½ years old. Two years can make a big difference in antler size.

= INDIVIDUALITY & AGING =

The coloration of these two bucks is considerably different, but both are within the normal range. Notice how even the velvet skin on their antlers is very different. Each whitetail has his own unique appearance because of a variety of factors. Without even considering antlers, there is a huge diversity of faces, markings, colorations, body-shapes, necks, noses, ears, eyes, and all of the various body parts which make up the picture. There is an almost infinite range of possibilities and combinations.

The white-tailed deer is an animal of many faces, both literally and figuratively. Whitetail enthusiasts tend to look at antlers so intensely, that many of them aren't paying much attention to the other parts of the animal. I'd have to agree that the mystique of the antlers alone is certainly enough to hold your interest, even in cases where you never get to see the rest of the animal. However, people who aren't paying close attention to the "whole" deer are really missing out on some interesting

and important information. Whitetails may be thought of as "herd" animals in some respects, but closer examination will reveal that they are actually very individualistic.

One of the things that continues to surprise me, as a serious observer and student of whitetails, is a question which I hear over and over again when discussing whitetail events and sightings — **HOW DO YOU KNOW IT'S THE SAME DEER THAT YOU SAW LAST YEAR? — OR LAST TIME?**

The situation for many people seems to be that if they can't recognize a buck by

111

There are as many different whitetail faces as there are whitetails. Once you start paying close attention, you will begin to see a great deal of difference from one deer to the next. Both of the two bucks above are obviously very old with their jowls and thick faces, but the shapes and details of their faces are very different. Each buck is easily recognizable, even without his antlers.

some very distinctive or unusual *antler* characteristic, then they don't recognize him at all. It's perfectly alright to look at antlers, but often it's the *face* that really tells the story. You can "know" a deer in the woods by his face, much the same as you would "know" a person that you've seen before. You can also recognize deer by their personalities, attitudes, colorations and many other attributes. It's generally quite easy to familiarize yourself with individual deer, but it helps to pay close attention to faces and other details.

We all have eyes, noses, mouths and ears. If you measured the differences in these characteristics, the variations would be miniscule in most cases. Nonetheless,

the small, subtle differences which do exist make each of us appear as a slightly different "face" and creates the "individual" look which each of us has. It's the same with whitetails. All deer don't have the same faces any more than people do. With just a quick glance, it might be easy to say that all deer look about the same, but that's only because we haven't trained ourselves to notice the details like we do with people. By paying closer attention to details in the field, you'll soon find that with very little effort you will be recognizing deer as easily as people. Familiar deer will begin to seem like old friends.

As a group, whitetails possess a very large array of different faces. Some are

The face on the buck at the left is downright strange-looking. His head is rounded and his eyes protrude. There's a lot of white around his eyes and nose, and the hair on his head is very thin. The buck at the right has a more squared head, floppy ears, a broader nose and an attractively marked face. If you take the time to study faces on bucks like these, you'll know them if you see them again.

inherently attractive, with nicely proportioned features and beautiful markings, and others are just plain ugly, with bug-eyes, broad faces, scruffy hair and dull markings. The white and black markings on whitetail faces vary tremendously. Some are very distinctive and sharp, with bright contrasts, as though they were just painted on with a brush. Others are dull and barely noticeable, with blacks which are almost gray and dirty whites.

The colors of foreheads also vary a lot, from a light gray, to almost white, to browns, tans and rust-colored hues, to some which are almost black. Many times I've heard people comment that a given buck "must be really old, because his forehead is so gray," but this is not necessarily the case. Some young deer have very gray faces, and some very old deer have dark, mahogany-colored faces. The colors are due to individuality more than age.

Some bucks have hardly any white at all on their muzzles, while others sport a distinct, white band behind their black noses. Some have black stripes at the sides of their jaws. There are a variety of patterns of white hair around the eyes. In a few cases there are white circles around the eyes as though the buck is wearing glasses.

There are bucks with squinty, almond-shaped eyes who look like they can hardly see. Then there are bucks with round eyes, and some with huge bug-eyes which look

The buck at the upper left has a white throat patch that starts at his chin and goes essentially all the way to his chest, which is unusual. The upper right photo shows a buck with no white throat patch at all. This also is quite unusual. The buck at the lower right has a distinct double throat patch. This is not such a rare occurrence, but his two white patches are particularly well-defined. The buck at the lower left has a classic, bright white, well-defined, single throat patch. There are many variations.

The two bucks above look different for a variety of reasons, but one of the most remarkable differences is their ears. The big buck on the left has relatively small and rounded ears. His ears also have black edges. The buck on the right has extremely long and somewhat pointed ears. The buck on the left has a double throat patch, while the other buck's throat patch is poorly defined.

as though they're about to pop out. Most deer have eyes which are dark brown to black, but once in a while some of them have amber-colored eyes. There are bucks with ears that are almost round, and others with very pointed ears. Ears can be very large or small. The "spread" of the ears, which is frequently used in estimating antler spread, varies considerably. A good average may be about 17 inches, but the spread can vary anywhere from about 14 inches up to about 20 inches, depending on the individual.

There are deer with long noses, short noses, broad noses, thin noses and "Roman" noses. Once again, if you actually measured them, the differences would be small. The difference between a "long" nose and a "short" nose may be only a couple of inches or less, but just as the size and shape of a human nose is a major feature used in recognition, so it is with deer.

Another major identifying characteristic is the white throat patch which most white-tails have. There are a few deer which have no discernable throat patch at all, but that's rare. The white throat patches may vary considerably in size, shape and intensity of color. Some are bright, pure white, while others are a dull, or cream-colored white. I've seen many different bucks which have *two* throat patches instead of one. There have been several times when I was watching deer, and oddly, I knew there was something different or strange about a buck's appearance, but I couldn't seem to put my finger on it. Then, it finally dawned on me that there was an extra throat patch. Some throat patches are so well defined that it looks as though they're outlined. On others the throat patch and the darker hair just seem to merge and fade around the edges. One fairly rare occurrence is a white patch which covers

These two bucks illustrate a number of facial differences, but the contrasts in their colorations are particularly interesting. The buck at the left has a very gray face with gray highlights, and the other is tan and brown with a rust-colored patch on his forehead. The buck on the right has smaller ears and his jowls are more prominent. Incidentally, look at the size of his left antler base!

the entire throat, extending from below the chin almost down to the chest. Overall, the white throat patch, against the contrasting darker throat, is a highly visible, important identifier, which many times can be seen (and identified) from long distances.

There are also major facial differences in bucks of different age classes. This is an important factor for a hunter or wildlife manager to know, so that it's possible to properly size up and compare different animals for management purposes. Generally, younger bucks will have relatively slender faces, with the lines of the nose and jaw appearing as a fairly straight line. As they age, the nose becomes thicker, sometimes with a hump, and the jaw becomes fuller. Prime faces are full, taut and muscular. As whitetail bucks age fur-

ther, the jaw usually becomes more pear-shaped, fuller, thicker, perhaps a little droopy. Some older bucks even develop a "dewlap," under their chin, like an old brahma bull. With chunkier features and looser skin, along with the bumps and scars of time and experience, some older bucks develop faces which are practically dripping with "character."

When you take the variability of all the different features of a whitetail's face into account, an almost infinite range of possibilities emerges. Sometimes you may recognize a particular whitetail with the identification of a single feature, but many more times you'll recognize him by a *combination* of features. It's usually the overall view which identifies him. Many times you'll be able to make the identification

*There may be times when you will have some difficulty concentrating on the **faces** of bucks. With bucks such as the two above, there is a tendency to see nothing but antlers. Nevertheless, their faces are likely to be more dependable standards for future recognition, because there's a chance their antlers will be grossly different in another year. Also, antlers will not tell you much about age.*

more absolute by combining facial recognition with other characteristics, such as antler shapes, body features and personality traits. Some deer even have a recognizable "gait" or walking posture.

Once a whitetail buck reaches the age of 3½, the "mainframe" of his antlers tends to be recognizable from year to year. While the number of points and the positioning of abnormal points may vary from year to year, the basic shape and form of the rack usually remains very recognizable. There are occasional exceptions to this concept, but not many.

Body shape, muscularity and coloration are also frequently recognizable. Many times the deciding factor for positive identification is in the personality and "attitude" of the buck. While some bucks may

Here's a face with a lot of character that will be easy to recognize. Don't rely on the unusual antler point for recognition, because it is a temporary injury that will probably correct itself next year.

The three bucks in the large photo just above are good examples of average or better 2½-year-old bucks. The 10-point buck at the upper left is a very exceptional 2½-year-old deer. The deer at the upper right is also a very exceptional 2½-year-old buck with 14 sturdy points, seven on each side.

This is a healthy 1½-year-old buck with his first set of antlers, a small eight-point rack. Normal yearlings may have antlers with anywhere from 2 to 12 points.

be partially recognizable by their "small" ears or by their "large" ears, they may be even more recognizable by the *manner* in which they customarily hold or present their ears. Some bucks seem to hold their ears at perpetual "attention," while others will usually let their ears "flop." Some are constantly flicking their ears as though they have a nervous "tick," and others tend to hold them at the horizontal position most of the time. It's the same with eyes. Some bucks are wide-eyed and constantly attentive, and others usually walk around with their eyes half closed, looking like they're sleepy all the time. When you put all these different factors together, the

All the bucks on this page are 3½ years old. This is the year when most bucks first really begin to show their stuff. Most bucks don't give you much of an idea about what to expect with their first two sets of antlers, but many times the third set will include characteristics that you'll see repeated in one variation or another for the rest of their lives. The buck at the upper left is showing height and stickers which he repeated thereafter. The buck on the right is exceptionally wide with short points, and he retained these features later on. The buck at the lower left is wide with double drop-tines, which is unusual on a buck this young.

sum total of each deer's unique qualities can make identification quite easy.

There currently is a great deal of effort being directed toward whitetail management. There are many factors involved in the production of large-antlered, mature bucks, and **nutrition, genetics and age** are paramount. Numerous management programs are in place throughout the country, and some are enjoying considerable success through habitat improvement, numbers management, supplemental feeding, etc. Upon reflection, it seems that almost every plan purportedly has its own special

These are 4½ -year-old bucks. At this age the bucks are just beginning to get a little meat on their bones and starting to show a little more character in their antlers. They are also in the process of becoming an entirely different animal. If they survive this season and go on to reach full maturity, they will be so different from the younger age classes, in terms of their behavior, that they might as well be another species. Compared to other age classes, the mortality rate of 4½ -year-olds is very high.

formula, or its own secret mix of "herbs and spices," so to speak. When all is said and done, most programs are actually quite similar and for good reason. There is no "magic bullet," no panacea. All programs essentially have the same management tools available to them, and even though they may try to run at it from many different directions, they're all running toward the same goal line. Various programs may be trying to fine tune the process with slightly different techniques, but in the end they're all trying to improve their herds primarily through nutrition, genetics and age.

After studying many different programs, there is one concept which rises above the others as the clear choice for the easiest

and most successful way to improve a herd. The concept is to **"Let 'em walk and watch 'em grow."** Far and away the simplest way to enhance overall antler quality is to refrain from harvesting deer until they reach maturity — at least five years of age or more. It sounds like the easiest thing in the world, but people have the hardest time following through with it. It takes a lot of resolve, patience and money.

Since the improvement of age structure is such an integral part of any management plan, it has become more important than ever to understand the whitetail aging process. Before either hunters or wildlife managers can assess a herd, and before either can properly crop or harvest from

Here are some prime examples of 5½ -year-old bucks. To my way of thinking, this is when real maturity begins for a whitetail buck. They have now filled out and muscled up somewhat, but they still have a smooth look overall. Also, now that their bodies have been built up, there is more nutrition available for antler growth, and in most cases it really makes a big difference. After having survived five seasons in a generally inhospitable world, they've learned much, including a multitude of ways to avoid human contact.

The bucks on this page are some old men of the woods. They are fully mature, in some cases downright ancient. For the most part, few humans would be much of a match for any of these well-experienced deer if they were to go up against them one-on-one in the woods. They know all the tricks. From the upper left, clockwise, they are believed to be 7½ , 6½ , 10½ and 8½ years old.

the herd, it is essential that they get a firm grasp on the concept of aging deer on the hoof. With practice, it can be done.

The best practice is to track some of the same bucks from year to year and see how they progress as they mature. It sounds simple enough, but if you're working mostly with wild, hunted deer as I am, then trying to find the same bucks for several years in a row can be a considerable problem . They tend to disappear for one reason or another. Some accidentally step in front of bullets, and others are involved in deer/auto accidents. A few are killed by other bucks, while some die of natural causes. Others become nocturnal, and many just disappear without a trace, never to be seen again. Tracking bucks year to year is a process with a very small percentage of success, but it's very educational.

The spectacle of year-to-year whitetail watching is growing, and it's becoming somewhat easier to accomplish on some lands as management programs allow more and more bucks to reach mature ages. In fact, the very concept of "whitetail maturity" is currently undergoing some philosophical changes. There was a time when a buck was considered to be "mature" at the age of 3½ in many circles. Later, much of the popular opinion changed the age of "maturity" to 4½ for most practical purposes. Even now, that premise is the basis for many management plans.

However, after having personally observed tens of thousands of different bucks, I have a different view of whitetail maturity. I saw many of these bucks only once, but others I saw repeatedly. In a few really fortunate instances (about 100 or so), I've been able to track the same buck from year to year — sometimes for only two or three years, but many times for four, five or six years, or even more. This has taken place in many different locations in a variety of different environments.

There are three different age classes represented here, and it's the same buck, three years in a row! This shows him at age 6½ at the top, 7½ in the center and 8½ at the bottom. This is proof positive that some mature bucks can continue to produce excellent antlers, even at advanced ages.

*The photographs on this page show **five consecutive years** in the life of a single buck. I first saw him at age 3½ in the photo at the upper left. He had a compact 10-point mainframe with small bumps showing on one brow-tine and his tallest tines. At the center left, at age 4½ , he had 10 well developed typical points and a split brow-tine on his right side. At age 5½ in the lower left picture, he grew a 10-point typical frame with a sticker point, but the split brow-tine moved to his left side. In the large picture, at 6½ , he had nine typical points with stickers on both sides and a split brow-tine back on his right side again. At 7½ , in the lower right photo, he had a slightly smaller nine-point mainframe with stickers on both sides and no split brow-tines.*

*The photo sequence above covers **seven seasons** in the life of one whitetail buck. There are only five photos because during two of the seven years I wasn't able to find him. In the upper left photo he is 3½ years old and carries a respectable eight-point rack. In the upper center photo he is 4½ years old, and for reasons unknown has grown a couple of odd drop-tine points along with a somewhat larger typical mainframe. At 5½ years of age, in the upper right picture, he has grown an extremely symmetrical and well developed 10-point rack. Though I tried, I couldn't find him during the season when he was 6½ years old, when he may have grown his largest set of antlers. At the lower left, he reappeared at age 7½ with 10 typical points, although one of the tines was very weak. I couldn't find him at age 8½, but in the lower right photo he showed up, at age 9½, with a rack similar to the one from two years before. He appeared to be in remarkably good health for his age. After seven seasons he seems like an old friend.*

*Here are **four consecutive years** in the life of a handsome buck. In the upper left photo he is 2½ years old with nine typical points. At the lower left he is putting on body weight at 3½ years of age, and he has grown a nice, compact 10-point typical rack. His typical frame has two small sticker points on his left side, one on his third point and one near the end of his beam. In the larger photo (upper right) he is just beginning to look mature at 4½ . He has once again grown his 10-point typical frame (a little larger) with the two sticker points on his left side. However, one of the sticker points has moved from his beam to his fourth point. He also had a couple of small burr points. At age 5½ (lower right) he grew a larger 10-point frame with a notch on one brow-tine, but no sticker points.*

I only saw this particular buck on two separate occasions. Oddly, it was a rainy, foggy day both times. I first saw him in the larger photo (on the right side). I judged him to be 4½ years old after studying him for a few minutes and watching him interact with some other deer. I saw him again two years later, at age 6½ (on the left), within 100 yards of the previous location. I thought it was remarkable how similar the proportioning and shape of his antlers had remained, even though they were now considerably larger.

Even considering whitetail individuality and regional differences, general patterns of development definitely do emerge. Whitetail bucks which are 1½ or 2½ years of age are strictly juveniles in any part of the country. Overall, whitetail bucks do not begin to "show their stuff" until they are at least 3½ years of age. Beginning with the third set of antlers you can generally start to see a given buck's antler potential. At 4½ years of age, some bucks are beginning to look extremely good, but I see very few examples of year-to-year development in which bucks do not improve their antlers substantially at age 5½. In fact, almost all improve their antlers again at age 6½. Plenty of them will grow even more impressive antlers at age 7½. There are always exceptions. I've seen two or three bucks which grew their best set of antlers at age 4½. I've also observed bucks which improved substantially at ages 8½, 9½ and even 10½. I believe that the latter exceptions are far more prevalent. In some cases the "old codgers" continued to grow impressive antlers for several consecutive years *after* reaching maturity. Some managers have made similar observations, and their programs are beginning to take this into account, as they keep increasing the ages in their definitions of "maturity."

Many old bucks are quite intriguing. When you examine the scars, lines and wrinkles of their faces, it often seems that, like old men, they must have quite a story to tell. And they probably do.

*There must be a million ways a whitetail can hide. For that matter, there are probably another million ways they can go unnoticed even when they're not really trying. Common whitetail habits which have evolved tend to keep them automatically out of harm's way. The buck in the top photo, bedded down during the middle of the day, is only visible from this specific angle with the help of the light-colored grass beyond. In the middle photo the drop-tine buck is acting cautiously, but not nearly so much as the larger buck which is holding back behind him in the brush. Did you see him? In the bottom picture, one of the bedded bucks has just stood up due to my unwelcome presence. Did you immediately see all **three** bucks? Anytime you see one buck, always look carefully for others.*

This buck is not hiding, but for all intents and purposes he might as well be. It sometimes seems that whitetail bucks are just as safe right out in the open as they are when they're hiding, simply because all their warning systems are so efficient. They are constantly watching, listening and smelling. You're no more likely to get close to this buck here than if he were in deep woods.

The huge whitetail buck stood like an apparition as I studied him intently with my binoculars. In an area noted for an overabundance of young, small-antlered deer, he seemed like a different species of animal, somehow magically transported from some other time or place.

Some would say it was an accident that I even saw him, but that may not be the case. "Luck" is always more than welcome around here, but experience has shown, time and time again, that the harder I work, the luckier I get. I had used the experience gleaned from many years of hunting to "accidentally" find this monster. Had I been less patient, or less thorough, I never would have seen him. I was working a brushline, glassing ahead and out toward the numerous small patches of cover which were spread over a broad, open area. The edge of the heavy brush seemed the most promising, but I knew from experience that it would not be unusual for a buck to choose to hide in one of the small islands of brush mixed among the scattered oak

Here are some examples of the whitetail security systems at work. It's a 24-hour-a-day process. The top photo shows two bucks working with a "buddy" system, more or less, each keeping an eye out for danger. The buck at the lower left is using his ears and eyes, and he's not likely to miss very much. The buck at the lower right is getting a nose-full of odor. These bucks may be out in the open, but they're reasonably safe. They're likely to see, hear or smell any predator and be long gone before the predator ever gets close.

trees. I hadn't seen anything but a jackrabbit in the last hour. But when I looked carefully into the shade of one of the small mottes, I noticed a straight horizontal shadow mixed in with a world of primarily vertical lines. It might have been nothing but a fallen or broken limb, but after a few minutes it moved and became the back of a whitetail doe. She trotted out into the open and back to the shade a couple of times, but there were no indications that other deer were present. However, the

The three photos on this page show an actual sequence that illustrates the various levels of concern and alarm that whitetails sometimes express. In the upper left photo, the buck hears something but is only mildly concerned. In the upper right shot, he has reached another level of concern. He seems to be taking it more seriously as he tries to listen more carefully. In the third photo, at the lower right, he has shifted to yet another, higher level of concern and is quite tense. All systems are on full alert. A moment later and he was out of there! I still had not heard or seen anything. Just after he was out of sight, several feral hogs ran into the clearing.

peak of the rut was nearing, and the timing was right that she might have company. She was mature, and though I may have imagined it, she seemed to be acting a little "squirrely" as does in estrus frequently do. I decided to watch her for a while. I sat motionless for over an hour, but nothing remarkable happened. She lay down and got back up a couple of times. It was very tempting to move on to greener pastures. I was watching all around, but mainly I kept trying to pry into the doe's lair with my 10-power binoculars. I was just about ready to give up, when I saw the smallest of movements in the grass behind the doe. When the monster buck stood up to

stretch, I could hardly believe my eyes. He had been there all along.

Seeing whitetails in their native habitat can be a very difficult task. The "art" of seeing deer in the woods is a hard-earned skill, which is best learned through the practice of actually seeing deer over and over again. You can practice elsewhere by trying to make yourself pay more attention to details. It takes an analytical, observant eye, and there may be ways of improving your powers of observation generally, but nothing else really compares to time spent in the woods actually watching real deer. That's why the people who are fortunate enough to spend a lot of time in the woods usually have a distinct advantage over others who get to the woods only occasionally.

Even the most experienced observers have to keep in practice. It's not as though you learn and then forget it.

When you're moving around in the deer woods, you're frequently being watched from the shadows, whether you realize it or not. Whitetails know instinctively that they are less likely to be noticed if they remain perfectly motionless. Many times, when they are standing still in the shadows, they can become almost invisible. Without the tiny shaft of light I might never have seen the bottom buck.

Rather, it's just that many of the nuances that you're searching for are so subtle that, without constant practice, you tend to lose your edge. Have you ever noticed how, after spending several days in the woods, your ability to "see" deer is dramatically improved on the last few days compared to the first day or two?

The conditions and situations in which we do our deer spotting are so diverse that total proficiency is out of the question. At times the deer are essentially "invisible." Further, it's not unusual for experienced people with excellent "deer eyes" to have times when they just can't see a particular

There was a time when many people believed that whitetails never looked up. It was thought that ambushing a whitetail from above should be as easy as falling off a log. Most everybody knows better now. The cautious nature of whitetails demands that they constantly be on the lookout for danger from every possible direction and every angle, including up.

deer that is plainly visible, even after having it pointed out to them. We all seem to have our good days and bad days.

By now, most people know that in trying to see whitetails in their natural cover, we should not expect to see the whole deer, at least not at first. We're actually looking for *parts*, certain parts, that when seen individually or in various combinations, spell

The key to seeing and recognizing the buck in the photo to the left is the triangle formed by the three black dots of the eyes and nose. Even so, he is difficult to see, and if you were very far away it would be almost impossible. Mature bucks have nerves of steel and patience to match, and that was proven by the buck at the bottom of the page. As I was driving down a ranch road at midday he ran across the road ahead of me. I stopped and followed his trail on foot, and this is what I found. After taking this photo I made some noise to try and force him to move, so that I might get a running shot. No amount of yelling, whistling or rock tossing would budge him, because he was so convinced that he had not been seen. He held tight, scrunched back under the brush until I literally walked up to him.

"D-E-E-R!" Naturally, we're straining to see anything that we can, but certain pieces of the puzzle are easier to interpret than others. The parts most commonly utilized in identifying deer in heavy cover would include the antlers, the legs, the eyes and nose, the continuous lines of the back and underside, the tail, the ears, and the white throat patch. Silhouettes and color patterns can also be very helpful in picking a hidden deer out of the brush. Obviously, combinations of any of the above make for a much more convincing identification.

With time and practice, you'll be able to memorize the shapes, patterns and colors

The bucks on this page are quite difficult to see, even though I have tightened up the pictures and zeroed in on them for you. In reality they were much harder to see in the woods. As always, you should look for bits and pieces of an animal rather than looking for the whole animal.

The use of cover is automatic for a whitetail buck. The buck in the above photo isn't drinking at all, as it appears. He is actually "hiding" beneath the branches. He held perfectly still in that position for about 10 minutes. The buck in the photo to the left is performing another version of the same behavior. Whitetails are constantly minimizing their exposure.

of all these parts on a detailed basis, perhaps even on a subconscious level. There have been many times when I've been walking or driving through the woods, when suddenly an alarm has gone off in my head. When it happens, all I know for sure is that I've just seen a deer, maybe eight steps back or maybe 50 yards back. I usually don't even know the spot where I saw the deer, but it's rarely a false alarm. Many times I can backtrack and either glimpse the fleeing animal or find the deer still concealed exactly where I passed it by. Sometimes it's hard to say what sparked the alarm — perhaps the glint of an antler, the triangular pattern formed by the eyes and nose, or maybe the shape of an ear.

The buck in the photo above has bedded in the middle of a clump of trees on a high hump. He has great visibility but can hardly be seen. Even when whitetails aren't actually hiding they can still be quite difficult to see, as illustrated by the buck in the photo on the right. He blends with the trees.

Many variables affect our ability to see deer, but probably none more than the varying types and intensities of available light. Since weather conditions and time of day are the primary causes of changes in light quality and intensity, these two factors can greatly alter our ability to see whitetails. The same deer, standing in the same location, observed from the same spot, will be seen quite differently as the sun moves across the sky and the shadows shift accordingly. While the deer may be very visible at 8 a.m., he could be quite difficult to see in the harsh light and mottled shade of 12 p.m., and he may be virtually invisible in the deep shade of 5 p.m. However, if cloud cover moves in during

The above buck exemplifies the concept of "hiding in plain sight." You'll see him quite easily, since I've narrowed down the field of view and focused in on him. But his natural colors blend so well with the landscape that he was quite difficult to see when looking at the overall scene. The other buck has chosen habitat which is so dense that it would be hard to see anything living there.

the morning, and the sky is lightly overcast at 12 p.m., the harsh light will now be moderated, the hard shadows will be gone, and the deer will be much more visible.

On sunny days, it's very important to keep the sun at your back as much as possible, especially very early and very late in the day. Moving directly into the sun during the first hour or so of sunrise or just before sunset is purely a losing battle.

Going after deer on cloudy days has both advantages and disadvantages. It's easier on the eyes, and the relative lack of shadows can reveal many deer that would be much more difficult to see if the sun was shining. At the same time less light means less color visibility, and sometimes

It was a cold November afternoon as this buck headed back into the heavy brush, probably to bed down. His body and face showed him to be only 3½ years old, but take a look at that rack! After a few more steps he was out of sight, and I didn't see him again. Can you imagine how many times we must walk within yards of monsters like this and never see them.

almost everything takes on a gray cast. The colors of everything, including the deer, may blend so well that differentiation becomes difficult. The darker the day, the more difficult the problem becomes.

The effects of rain and fog are self-evident, but these conditions can sometimes be used to your advantage. Even though your visibility is much diminished, so is that of the deer. It may be that the rainiest, nastiest, foggiest days are the days when you and the deer will be on the most even terms where visibility is concerned.

There is a wide range of challenges to be met in learning to see deer, not the least of which is their amazing adaptability. Even

when there is no place to hide, they can usually find a way. We've all heard of bucks who laid on their bellies with their chins flat on the ground in order to hide in the grass as intruders passed by. I was recently following a buck across a wide open pasture when he just disappeared into thin air. After analyzing the situation from every angle, I finally found him in a drainage ditch, hiding from me. He was scrunched tightly under a small bridge. Whitetails will fool you, trick you, get away from you, and mostly, never be seen by you in the first place.

Green weeds + blooming flowers + velvet = summertime. What a sight to see as I came over a hill in my truck on an August morning! He stood there just long enough for a couple of quick shots with a 500mm lens. He's gorgeous, but he doesn't look nearly as masculine as he will in the next few months. Over the next 90 days or so, he will become a different animal.

 **CHANGING OF THE COLORS** =

Most fawns are born in late spring and early summer. After just a few weeks of life they are leaping and bounding with the big boys, like the young fawn in the top photo. On the June morning when I took the bottom photo, I had been watching a brushline for some time when I noticed a bit of movement in a big field of tall weeds. When I began glassing with my binoculars, the weeds came alive with the tips of antlers. These bucks were probably bedded in the weeds. I can see at least eight different bucks in the bachelor group.

Relentless posturing and kicking goes on throughout the summer, as shown in the top photo. It's interesting, in the center shot, that the big mature buck grows his much larger antlers in the same amount of time that the yearling grows his tiny ones. At the bottom left a handsome 12-pointer takes an early morning drink. The buck at the lower right is feeding on a hilltop as the sun rises behind him.

*The most exciting thing about summertime whitetails is — **bachelor groups**! As the top photo shows, a lot of whitetail activity during this period is associated with water. Much of this activity takes place just about sunrise and again at sundown. In the bottom picture a very impressive bachelor group has bedded down in the shade. These are the kinds of sights that will make your heart leap.*

As summer begins to come to an end, the antlers are fully grown and the velvet begins to dry out as the antlers finish the hardening process. The bucks are very impressive this time of year with their thick velvet antlers. In late summer the bucks become increasingly antagonistic toward each other, as in the top photo. The fat buck running at the lower left is in the midst of changing from his summer coat to his winter coat. The buck at the bottom right has already begun performing scraping behavior while in velvet.

I surprised the three bucks in the top photo as they fed on an open hill. As summer comes to an end the bucks come out of velvet, one by one. Some bucks, such as the split-beamed buck at the middle left, don't do a particularly good job of cleaning the velvet off. They may wear shreds for days or even weeks. As you can see, all bucks don't take the velvet off at one time. In the middle right picture the big 6x7 has removed his velvet while the smaller buck has not. In the bottom photo, about half of the bachelor group is out of velvet.

In early fall many of the bachelor groups hold together for a while, but usually not for long. The bucks in the top photo are all fairly equal in terms of antlers. The middle shot, taken just at sundown, shows a monster nine-pointer leaping the fence as two younger 10-pointers follow. The four bucks at the bottom were bedded down, but jumped up and ran as I approached them.

As fall finally arrives the bachelor groups have mostly split up, and the bucks have practically become different animals. Their systems are beginning to run hot with testosterone and they'll soon be going nuts as the pre-rut period kicks in. The bucks at the upper left and on the right are relatively young deer, perhaps 3½ or 4½ years of age. The lower left buck may be past his prime.

As the pre-rut period begins, whitetail bucks start to increase their activities substantially. The big 12-pointer at the top of the page is performing classic scraping behavior. At the left he is smelling, chewing, licking and rubbing the "licking branch" in order to leave his personal scent, as well as to test the branch for the scents of others that have been there. At the right he is pawing out a clean area with his hoof, and urine will be deposited there. It's also about this time that bucks begin to get into more and more scuffles.

As the rut approaches, mature bucks begin to move around more and more, checking out new doe groups and trying to maintain or improve their social status. Though they've been making rubs throughout the fall, this activity may be increased as well. Soon, big bucks that have never been seen before will start coming out of the woodwork as the competition heats up. Expect anything!

With every passing week the bucks seem to be more anxious, and they are definitely becoming less tolerant of any other bucks which cross their paths. By now they are traveling far beyond the boundaries of their normal range, looking for any does which might be coming into estrus. It's an exciting time to be in the woods. All kinds of behaviors are being carried out to the extremes.

One of the most common behaviors to be seen is the so-called "lip-curling," technically known as the flehmen behavior. It is performed in several different situations, but the most common is when a buck comes to a spot where a doe has urinated. He will taste the ground or grass and raise his head back, savoring the odors. This stimulates and primes his sexual libido.

*Once the first few whitetail does actually come into estrus, the bucks fairly well lose their minds. As you can see, all the bucks on this page are single-mindedly going about the now-serious business of following the scent trails of does. They go after them morning, noon and night with their noses to the ground just like bird dogs. Bucks will frequently ignore **everything** else but the scent trail.*

During the rut, bucks will continue to make new scrapes and rework old ones in an effort to predominate and be as widely known as possible. On the one hand they want the does to be aware of their presence, and on the other they want to intimidate the other bucks. The buck on the left is working a licking branch that is so high he has to stand erect and hop up to reach it.

The bucks are now hanging very close to the doe groups, and when they find a doe that is in estrus, or smells like she's about to be in estrus, they guard her quite literally with their life. They will continuously dog her and rush her to determine the status of her readiness. They're likely to stay very close, perhaps within 10 yards or so, and will follow her wherever she goes.

Once a buck has definitely located a doe in heat, he will stick with her like glue for as much as a couple of days. He likely will not eat, drink or go anywhere without her. Any other bucks which approach her will be met with extreme prejudice. With all of the incredible repertoire of behaviors and preparations for the rut, the actual breeding process is usually quite brief, perhaps lasting only 10 or 15 seconds. The photo at the lower right is yet another good example of whitetail unpredictability. I was at a ranch headquarters a little after noon when this buck and doe ran out of the heavy brush and did their deed in the middle of the dirt road.

As fall becomes winter, breeding activity falls off. There are a few flurries of action with the secondary cycles of the few does which were not bred during the main rut. Survival becomes an important issue as available foods are consumed and the weather becomes more severe. As the winter wears on, the bucks start to regroup and get a little less antagonistic with each other.

By the time winter is over, many of the whitetails, especially the bucks, have really taken a beating. Months of traveling far, chasing does and fighting other bucks takes its toll. During the height of the season, the bucks get so carried away that they just don't bother to take the time to eat. Then later, when they desperately need the nutrition, the food is not readily available. Both bucks at the top of the page have lost a tremendous amount of weight. The two at the bottom didn't survive the season.

In my work as a whitetail photographer I come across a wide variety of other animals along the way. Some of the most common deer (other than whitetails) that I see are the fallow deer, originally of European origin. They have been imported to many locations in the United States over the last 50 years or so. In parts of the southwest these deer and many other varieties of the so-called "exotics" have escaped so often and reproduced so extensively that they are commonly seen on open range.

⸺  WHITETAIL SIDETRACKS =

I was traveling hurriedly across this pasture just before sundown to get to another location where I had been feeding whitetails. I heard a loud cracking noise and turned to see these two blackbuck antelope fighting on the hilltop under a rising full moon. It was a unique scene and an unexpected opportunity. The moon rises during the few minutes before sundown only a few times each year, regardless of the moon phase, and some of those days are cloudy. The possibility of photographing any animal in this scene is exceedingly rare. Even when all the variables do come together, the window of opportunity is only a handful of minutes.

The pursuit of whitetails is, in effect, its own reward, which is to say, "If you play the game at all, you win!" The majority of people who go out after deer get a great deal of satisfaction from the chase itself and also from the other adventures that are inevitable in the deer woods. Everybody wants to come back with a monster buck, or at least a monster-buck story, and most are working hard toward that end, but it's the overall experience which keeps us coming back again and again, even if we find deer only infrequently.

The overall experience actually encompasses much more than just the whitetails themselves. It's impossible to spend much time chasing after deer without stumbling into countless other animals and outdoor experiences — the "whitetail sidetracks," as I call them. Nothing else outscores the whitetails, but over time you're bound to

159

The whitetail experience, in and of itself, is a very rich experience. However, there is an almost endless variety of other animals which are also a part of the overall enjoyment. Whitetails share their habitat with many interesting creatures, and if you spend a lot a time pursuing deer, you're bound to see plenty of things that you never expected. The young coyote at the top didn't seem to know what to do with the armadillo. He finally just walked away. The jackrabbit in the middle went smoothly through a hole which seemed much smaller than he was. The bottom photo, taken during a drought, is the only time I've ever seen an armadillo drink from a pond, and he came for three afternoons in a row as I sat in a deer blind.

see some mighty interesting things, some with deer involved and some that have nothing to do with deer. Over time you'll come to cherish the memories of many of your "sidetrack" experiences almost as much as your whitetail memories. In fact, they are so inexorably tied together, that it's hard to separate one from the other.

From the standpoint of photography, the presence of other animals can be either a blessing or a curse, depending on the situation. There are mornings when I go through a lot of effort to get up, out and in position for a gorgeous sunrise, but there's not a whitetail in sight. At that point I'm glad to see almost anything appear on the hill — a coyote, turkey, jackalope, anything! On the other hand, there are mornings when everything is working, there's a nice whitetail buck on the hill and it will be sunrise in a few minutes. And here comes an axis deer or a cow to run the whitetail off just before the photo is possible. Such interruptions seem to be the rule rather than the exception.

Some of the most interesting sidetracks are the ones which include interactive behavior between a whitetail and a completely different species of animal. Generally, whitetails are pacifists when it comes to dealing with animals other than their own kind. They usually try to avoid most other animals, particularly those which have an aggressive nature or those which are large in stature. Needless to say, it's the exceptions that get your attention. The photos on this page are good examples. I've watched deer for years in areas which harbor large populations of feral hogs. Feral hogs are just about as aggressive as any animal in the woods, and worse than that, they can also

In many parts of the country, whitetails live in areas with large feral hog populations. Feral hogs are one of the most outwardly aggressive animals in the woods, and they've got the size, speed and weaponry to back it up. In most instances when a whitetail is confronted with even a small hog, the deer will immediately flee in terror. However, as you can see, there are exceptions.

grow to enormous sizes, in some cases upwards of four or five hundred pounds! Probably 99 times out of 100, *any* whitetail which encounters *any* hog at close range will run as though his tail were on fire. However, once in a while there is that fearless individual, a whitetail buck which shows absolutely no fear of feral hogs. I've also watched whitetails interact with many other types of animals, some fearsome like the hogs and others much more harmless.

As you can see from the examples in this chapter, I've come across a large variety of different animals in my quest for whitetails. Of course this shows only a few of them. Some of these photos are examples of situations which I've seen repeatedly, but many of the situations here are

The three bucks at the top of the page are not whitetails, but even the most jaded whitetail "nut" would surely have to stop and gasp slightly at the size of the antlers on the three fallow bucks. I did! All three are enormous. There is stiff competition between whitetails and fallow deer, and the fallows are usually more dominant. I've seen whitetail bucks and fallow bucks actually fighting.

essentially unique. Several of these are scenes that might *never* be observed again.

One of the animals that I seem to run into the most frequently is the coyote. I've had many interesting experiences with these highly intelligent characters. Among the most unusual is the situation pictured at the top of page 160, where the young coyote was trying to figure out how to deal with an armadillo. The coyote got so frustrated that he began pulling it around backwards by the tail. Finally, he took one last quizzical look at the four-legged bowling ball and just walked away.

One of the most thrilling experiences in the woods is to hear the joyous "group howls" of a pack of coyotes. In areas with heavy coyote populations, one pack is frequently joined by others howling in the distance. It *can* be a little disconcerting when you're sitting silently under a bush in some remote spot, and a group breaks into their musical cacophony only a few bushes over. Even so, its a sound that I really enjoy.

There have been times when I was watching deer and had the opportunity to

Whitetails and wild turkey share common ground throughout the country. Turkey are just about as consumed by the dominance factor as whitetails. The two toms at the upper left are very serious about it. The photo at the upper right poses the question ...Is this a really tall turkey or an extremely short deer?

Javelina (collared peccary) are fairly common animals in many parts of the southwest. They are small but relatively aggressive animals, with a large boar weighing perhaps 40 to 50 pounds. Whitetails that live in close proximity to them will usually try to avoid them, probably due to their pushy, aggressive nature. There are a few deer such as the one above which show little or no fear.

see coyotes actually stalking the deer before me. None of them ever came close to getting the deer. There have been other times when I stared in amazement as coyotes and deer stood around together in close proximity, with neither fear nor predatory intent apparent. My biggest surprise came when I saw a coyote come out of the brush and actually start eating corn about five yards from a yearling buck which was doing the same. They ate together for at least 10 minutes!

It seems to have become more and more common for coyotes to respond to deer-calling routines. I don't know if this is a

reflection of increased deer predation by coyotes or not, but I've almost been run over by them several times when I was either rattling antlers or using a grunt call. And these were not tentative responses. In one example I was rattling on a densely foggy morning when two coyotes came barreling out of the fog directly at me. They could barely keep from running into me as they veered off and started backpeddling at a range of perhaps three or four yards. Even then, when I started rattling again, one of them came back again, sat on his haunches, and began "barking" at me like a dog from 10 yards away. I've had a great

There is a huge diversity of birds in the woods and you'll have many opportunities to observe them as you wait for whitetails. The photo at the upper left shows a red-tailed hawk being hounded by a mockingbird. Mockingbirds, shrikes, kingbirds and several of the flycatchers are relentless in their persecution of the hawks. The blue heron at the upper right was hunting in a pond as I was watching deer from a nearby blind. I watched as he successfully caught his dinner, a leopard frog. The photo of the egret at the bottom is just one of thousands of beautiful and interesting sights I've seen while I was out after deer.

Coyotes are one of the most common predators in the deer woods. Whitetails will usually go well out of their way to avoid them, although there are times when they are practically ignored. Some people view coyotes with disdain but they are highly intelligent, very resourceful animals. And there's nothing quite like hearing a pack of coyotes breaking into a spontaneous "group-howl" while you're sitting silently, waiting for deer. I've watched them at great length as they went about their business or as they occasionally stalked the very deer I was watching. The smaller gray fox (at the left) is also very common, but I see them much less frequently.

many interesting encounters with the ubiquitous coyotes. The woods would be a poorer place without their presence.

I've also had many run-ins with feral hogs. Populations of wild hogs have grown tremendously in recent years. As recently as 20 years ago, I had never even seen one. Now, I see literally hundreds of them each season, and in some areas I can see hundreds of them in a week! As previously mentioned, hogs are just about as aggressive as any animal in the woods, and as such, they are a force to be reckoned with.

I don't live in constant fear of them when in the woods, but they have been known to injure and/or kill people, so they bear watching. Several of my rancher friends had told me of their destructive nature and aggressive attitude for years before I saw my first one. Even so, I commonly plowed my way through heavy brush on remote ranches, never giving much thought to the hogs. Never having seen one, I had almost begun to think of them as mythical beasts.

Then, late one October afternoon I was sitting in a tree trying to photograph deer as they traveled down a creek drainage. I was watching a couple of deer when I heard a noise behind me and turned to see six small feral hogs coming over a rise,

A number of ranches where I photograph deer also have elk. The aggressive bull elk in the upper right photo has broken off about half of his massive rack — and look at that drop-tine! The bull below is a very rare, completely white elk.

turning over rocks as they came, looking for food. I remember looking at the small "pigs" and thinking to myself — "So this is what fearsome feral hogs look like!" I turned back toward the deer in the creek and all but forgot about the little hogs.

It's really interesting how your instincts can start working for you, once you get into what some people would call a more "primitive" frame of mind. When you start functioning as an element of the natural world, your senses just begin to work differently. At any rate, after watching the deer for a few minutes, I became acutely aware that something was behind me, even though I had heard nothing. When I turned, I *knew* something would be there. I just didn't know what it would be. I certainly didn't realize that it would be the "mama" hog, all 300 pounds of long-nosed,

The spotted deer at the upper left is an axis deer, originally from Asia. They are one of the most common and numerous of the various imported deer species which thrive in many areas of the country. Axis deer are usually a little larger than whitetails and compete with them for food when they share the same territory. They're slightly more aggressive and usually dominant over whitetails.

black-haired, big-toothed, bad attitude that she was. I had never seen an animal with such an aggressive posture and such quick, jerky movements. I had no weapon, and the situation became a little desperate with darkness closing in. The seven hogs disappeared exactly between me and my truck, which was hidden in the brush about a quarter mile away. There was barely enough light to see, so it was time to make a move. I must have looked quite the fool as I ran from tree to climbable tree, sprinting 50 to 100 yards at a time, then looking for hogs and/or the next tree, until finally I reached the truck. I didn't see the hogs on the way, and I was glad. Since that time, I've had a great many encounters with wild hogs, often at close range, and I'm not nearly so fearful as before. Even so, it's amazing how often the last thing I see just before total darkness is a giant feral hog between me and safety.

Many of the unusual animals that I see in the woods wouldn't have been there at

For sheer entertainment value it's hard to beat the common black-tailed jackrabbit. They're always amusing to watch, and, as in the top photo, you just never know where they're going to show up.

Whitetails often try to avoid sheep when they are present in large numbers, but one-on-one they don't pay much attention to them. The photo at the left shows two blackbuck antelope. They are small animals, with beautiful markings and impressive horns. They have a variety of curious behaviors, much like whitetails do.

all 50 years ago, There are many varieties of the so-called "exotics," species native to Africa, Asia and Europe, that have been imported to numerous locations in the United States over the last 50 years or so. In parts of the country, especially areas in the southwest, many of these species have escaped so often and reproduced so extensively that they are commonly seen on open range. They have in effect become natives. I can still remember the first time I heard the "scream" of an axis buck in rut. It sounded as though someone was most certainly dying a horrible death in the next pasture. I never dreamed a deer could make a sound like that! I can also recall a time in the woods when I heard what seemed to be the roar of a mountain lion. When I cautiously made my way through

Whitetails usually are not afraid of blackbuck antelope, with their small stature, although I have seen them threaten each other a few times. The photo at the right shows a highly uncommon situation. The whitetail is aggressively threatening a much larger female waterbuck antelope. Whitetails are usually intimidated by size, but not this time.

the brush toward the repeated roars, I was amazed to find myself face to face with a fallow buck which was heavily into the rutting process. Even the sika deer, originally from Asia, caused me some distress at first. Several times when I was stalking silently through the woods I was a little *too* successful and sneaked right up on top of a sika deer. Their customary response to such an

It's always highly unusual when two separate species actually fight, as with the sika deer and the axis deer in the top photo. One of the most interesting animals of the southwest is the roadrunner. The one in the middle photo is living up to his name as he strides down the edge of the pavement. The bottom picture shows a pair of collared lizards, or "mountain boomers," as they are called.

I watched these massive, beautiful thunderheads building, towering over the hilltop, as I sat in a blind. It was almost like a living, breathing thing as it developed. As the photo at the bottom left illustrates, there are many small but wonderful sights in the undisturbed woods. In my line of work I have to keep a constant watch for the unwelcome situation at the bottom right.

*The photo at the top of the page shows "Albert," a German wirehaired pointer who is trained to point and retrieve birds, trail wounded deer and **to find and fetch shed antlers**, among other things. The shed antler in the bottom photo has been chewed by rodents or other small animals.*

intrusion is to jump up and shriek and whistle like nothing else you've ever heard. It'll make you almost jump out of your skin!

As you can see, there is a broad range of "sidetrack" experiences to be had. During one of the years when I was hunting and photographing in Mexico, there was an unusually large amount of mountain lion activity. That is to say, they were killing deer right and left on the 10,000 acre ranch where I was staying. Over 20 kills were found in only a two or three week period, including one about 100 yards behind the camp. Even so, no lions had actually been sighted, so it was assumed that most of the movement was nocturnal.

One day as I was exploring some heavy brush about two miles from camp, I found an area which was perhaps 40 yards in diameter, and it was filled with buck rubs and breeding scrapes. There must have been at least 30 small trees broken off in the circular area, and some of them were green and fresh. It looked like a great place to find a big buck, and I carefully made mental notes of the landmarks as I walked out, so that I could find my way back in the morning. About 4:30 a.m., I walked back to the spot while it was still dark. It was a perfect, icy-cold, still morning. As soon as there was enough light to see, I begin my rattling routines, but to no avail. I sat and waited for several hours, but nothing happened. I walked out by the same route I used going in, and I was more than a little surprised to find the *very fresh* head and rib-cage of a large, mature whitetail doe not far from the place

There are countless, priceless treasures to be found in the deer woods, and it's all an important part of the whitetail experience. Rocks, gems, Indian and early American artifacts, bones, antlers, fossils and any number of other things abound, just waiting to be discovered. There is a broad array of birds, reptiles, small animals and other life-forms practically begging to be seen. The more you discover and learn about all these things, the stronger your connection to the past and to the natural world.

where I'd been sitting. I had walked within five yards of it in the dark. It's no wonder I didn't see any deer! I had quite a tendency to look over my shoulder during the remainder of the trip.

I've had many other sidetrack experiences. There was the time when I stepped over a log while walking down a game trail just before dark. The "log" was an eight or nine foot indigo snake, as big around as a six-inch pipe, and I most certainly did the "dance of the wildflowers" when it moved. How about the morning just last season when I sat motionless in a blind, as three red cardinals flew in the window and flitted back and forth *inside* the blind with me.

Not all sidetracks are so pleasant, such as the time I ran over a shed antler with my truck, puncturing *both* right-hand tires in one fell swoop. Luckily I had two spares.

It's easy to get sidetracked by the many inanimate objects in the deer woods. I'm always fascinated by the wide variety of artifacts to be found, especially by the flint tools and arrowheads made by unknown men, hundreds or even thousands of years ago. You can't help but wonder about the people who made these wonderful, functional works of art. They may have pursued whitetails with some of these points, long ago.

"THE CROSSING"

In photographing whitetails and other wildlife, many different strategies are employed. The preparation can be complex and is often dependent on many variables, particularly the weather. Failures and dry runs are the norm, with a few marginal successes thrown in.

Then, once in a great while, everything works. The clouds dissipate and the sun comes out. The wind lays down. The cows or goats don't follow you to your blind, for once. You didn't forget the film or any of the equipment, and you're in position on time. And things actually begin to happen!

The photos shown on this page are excerpts from one of those rare days. I had been working in the area for over a week, and had been plagued by overcast skies, intermittent rain and high winds. Finally, a weather front had pushed through and a cold, blue norther had cleared the skies and left them sparkling clean.

In scouting around the five-digit acreage of this ranch I had located several concentrations of deer, but there was one location that particularly interested me. There was a large area of heavy, thick brush and scrub oak where there seemed to be an exceptional amount of activity. From a distance I had repeatedly seen whitetails coming out of the brush and jumping a fence at the top of a hill on the way to a food plot below. I had studied the places where they were coming over the fence and zeroed in on one spot in particular which seemed to carry a large amount of traffic. There was no blind or stand there, so I had picked out a thick bush and hollowed out a hole in it so I could sit on the ground there and watch down the fenceline toward the crossing spot.

As soon as it was light, I began seeing deer, and for a while it seemed like Grand Central Station. Whitetails began coming out of the woodwork like ants. The bad weather had kept them generally down for the last couple of days, and now they were frisky, hungry and on the move. As you can see by these examples, there was quite a variety of animals coming over the fence. The wild turkey hen in the top photo was just one of about a dozen turkeys that came over. The second photo from the top is indicative of the lateness of the season. This deer is a buck which has already shed his antlers. If you look closely you can see one antler pedicel. There was a variety of mostly small bucks that jumped the fence, along with does, fawns and even a couple of axis deer. The buck in the bottom photo has misjudged the height of the fence, and is jumping much higher than necessary. That's a really unusual thing to see. Whitetails are rarely off by that much.

When I returned to "The Crossing" the following season, I didn't see a single deer come over the fence. Such is whitetail photography.

BEHIND THE PICTURES

This is one of my favorite photos, at least partly because of the mood it evokes. It fairly reeks of drama, mystery and suspense. I guess I also like it because I had to work so hard to earn it. People generally have no idea of all the effort involved in producing images of wild deer like this. I spent over a week alone on a 30,000 acre ranch to get this and just a few other nice shots. I slept in a hunter's cabin and ate out of a sack in my truck. Each morning I got up before 5 a.m. and drove for miles down rut roads to get in the general vicinity of my target locations. I would then quietly load myself down like a pack mule and walk the last half mile in the dark, all the while wondering about the large feral hog population. When I reached my blind, sweating in the near-freezing temperature, I would quickly and quietly whisk the scorpions out of the blind and get my equipment set up. Then, the long wait for daylight would begin. Several mornings I sat silently in my cramped blind until noon without seeing a single deer. On the morning above, the fog was so thick that I could only see about 20 yards during the first hour of light. I could see shapes in the fog but couldn't identify most of them. There was so much moisture swirling in the air that my 500mm lens kept getting coated with it. A small eight-point buck walked within five yards of me, never stopping. After sunrise the fog began to open up a little, and the mature buck above materialized out of the swirling mists. He was cautious beyond words. I only got three or four quick shots of him, and he was gone forever. I sat there for three more hours without seeing a deer, then went to my truck for something to eat before I started the process all over again ...and again ...and again ...

Sometimes it seems that people are more interested in *how* I got the pictures, than in the pictures themselves. There's really no big secret to producing good whitetail photographs. It's difficult work, but if a person has enough desire to succeed, it can be done. The job requires hard work and a willingness to sacrifice comfort and convenience. It frequently demands that you put your other life aside in order to focus more intensely on the challenges at hand. Most people probably would be surprised at the amount of effort

involved. To do the job well calls for a lot of self-discipline and goal orientation, and it's necessary to commit to some standard of excellence. This is a little difficult in the beginning, because most photographers have to experiment considerably before the true nature of "excellence" becomes fully apparent. What seems "excellent" in the early stages usually is regarded as "junk" later on, as progress is made. A person must also be willing to go through great "extremes" in order to create good photographs — extreme patience, persistence, frustration, etc.

Whitetail photography is more of a thinking man's game than what some people realize. It would be great if it were possible just to go out and get the pictures, but it doesn't work quite that easily. The animals, the weather and the circumstances rarely work in your favor. You

Whitetails are out there, come rain or shine. They've got no place to go when it rains, so you might as well go after them. Generally, I find that whitetails will move around quite a bit in a drizzle or slow rain. Usually, when a heavy rain breaks out, whitetails will lay down or stand in cover until it passes. Both of the bucks above were actively moving and feeding in driving rain.

Bad weather is an integral part of the outdoor experience. The top photo on this page serves as a stark reminder for me. I took that shot as I came over a hill on a remote ranch where I was working. The weather had been terrible, and it had rained for eight days in a row. I had been out in it every day, from before daylight until dark, trying to wait it out. There had been a temporary clearing this particular afternoon, but, as you can see, there was a massive thunderstorm building up in the east. At dark I went back to my cabin to eat a sandwich and go to bed. I was physically and mentally exhausted. I'd seen some great bucks, but the days had been so dark that most of the time photography was just not possible. No one lived on the ranch and I was staying there alone. Shortly after I hit the sack and went to sleep, I awoke to the sounds of thunder and lightning followed by the sound of a driving rainstorm. I was almost glad, since I was so exhausted. It was already so muddy that I could hardly walk in the woods. Another night of this might make it impossible. I drifted back to sleep, awakened from time to time by another loud clap of thunder. When my alarm went off at 4:30 a.m. it was still pouring. As I reached to the floor to turn the alarm off, I put my hand into several inches of water. Now that's a wake-up call! The cabin was located near a small dry creekbed. Not anymore! The creekbed had turned into a raging brown river that reached out to encompass my cabin and another 100 yards uphill with three to four feet of roaring dirty water. My anxiety crested, and so did the water after about an hour. The area had received about 11 inches of rain that night alone, on top of another 10 inches or so the previous week. It had created unprecedented flooding. My troubles were still not over. From the cabin to the pavement was eight miles of very rough road which would be almost impassable after the flood. Also, there was a low-water crossing of a major creek just before getting to the highway. I was sure the creek would be impassable, so I didn't even try to get out right away. The second day I loaded up and headed for the highway well before first light. The dirt road was filled with downed fences, boulders and chug-holes the size of bathtubs. Finally, I made my way to the low-water crossing in the dark. There was no way! A muddy gravel bar had washed up over the road and there was still three to four feet of rapidly moving water. I had to go back into the ranch. I was trapped with no way out. I worked on repairing some of the downed fences for about half a day, and then went back to the low-water crossing. It was still risky, but I decided to give it a try. I barely made it across to freedom. I don't believe I was ever so glad to get off a ranch.

Much of my work is done out of deer blinds such as the ground blind in the background of the upper photo. That particular location actually has two blinds and I took this photo from the other blind. The photo to the left illustrates that you just never know what you're going to see. I was supposedly alone in the middle of a 40-square-mile ranch, 20 miles from the nearest small town. I'd been in a deer blind all afternoon when I saw seven men (probably illegal aliens) walk out of the brush. They passed by me at about 50 yards, oblivious to my presence. I snapped this photo of the last two just before they went out of sight. Such an experience is possible anywhere within a few hundred miles of the Mexican border. The bottom photo shows one of the many off-season residents of deer blinds. You never know what to expect when you go to clean out blinds in the early fall. This young great horned owl was just about ready to fledge and was able to fly away.

have to make them work for you! You do this by studying hard to get a thorough understanding of the variables involved and an accurate perception of the manner in which each variable will affect your photograph. Then you plan accordingly. If deer aren't presenting themselves in the location you want, change their travel plans. Make them go where you want them. Place a log across the unwanted route. Hang dirty shirts in the places where you don't want them to be. Park your truck in the oat patch where you don't

Many deer blinds are located in association with watering holes and/or feeding stations. The wide-antlered buck above is coming to a corn feeder. It seems that there is an endless array of disruptive factors when trying to hunt, watch or photograph deer from a blind. The photo to the right shows an all too common circumstance. Deer that you may have waited hours or even days to see, are frequently run off by domestic animals such as these horses. I've had many a promising photo shoot ruined by horses, cows, goats, sheep, hogs, javelina, coyotes, dogs, cowboys and many other factors.

want them to go. The options are almost endless, and the more you "think" about it, the more strategies you can come up with.

A great deal of whitetail photography is achieved through trial and error. Through experience, you learn what is possible, in terms of the equipment, your own abilities and the animals themselves. What's important is that you *understand and remember* what went right and what went wrong, so that you can capitalize on that knowledge the next time out. It's really that simple.

Some things you learn fairly easily. You don't have to get caught in the middle of nowhere in a driving rainstorm very many times to learn to always carry garbage bags

The photos on this page illustrate some of the common challenges faced in getting nice, natural photographs of wild whitetails. A big buck had been seen in this vicinity frequently, but the feeder was stark in the middle of a narrow sendero cut through the heavy brush. The feeder was surrounded by a pipe fence to keep the livestock from it. As you can see there were no attractive photos to be taken around the feeder, yet it was the reason for the concentration of deer there. I tried feeding by hand away from the feeder, along the edges of the sendero and in a small clearing which I had opened up with a machete. As the top photo shows, the big buck and another came to the feeder the first morning, but ignored the hand-fed areas because cows had found them first. I didn't get any usable photographs of him that day. I didn't see him at all the second or third day, but viewed him from a distance on the fourth day. On the fifth morning he showed up at the feeder, followed the trail of corn and found the feed in the small clearing. He stayed there for about two minutes, until another more dominant buck came and ran him away from the area. I kept coming back to my small temporary blind every morning for over a week. He returned twice but was chased away by hogs on one occasion and crowded out by cows on the other. I never did get any great shots, but with persistence I was able to come up with a few usable photos.

I saw the big, rutting buck above as I was driving toward a blind where I intended to sit for the afternoon. When I first watched him with binoculars he was chasing a doe across a 50 acre oat field, some distance away from my blind. I'd never seen him before. I knew the travel patterns of the area pretty well, and the way they were heading, they weren't very likely to show up in the vicinity of my blind. I decided that I would try to "drive" him toward the place where I would be. I eased up and parked my truck in a very visible location to the west of the buck. I felt he would not go to the east as it was a wide open area. I ran through the brush in a wide circle to approach the oat patch from the south, hoping to drive him north into a large brushy area. I knew that late afternoon deer traffic through that area might bring him to my blind at the waterhole. Sure enough, when I walked into the oat patch he started running to the west, and when he saw the truck he turned to the north. I could only hope for the best. I quickly got back to the truck and took it to a hiding place in the brush about a half mile from the blind. I walked to the blind and got set up, and a little before sundown the big 12-pointer showed up. It was the only time I ever saw him, but I was able to put him on a couple of magazine covers.

or some way of protecting your equipment, if not yourself. I've spent more hours huddled in ramshackle blinds during thunderstorms than you might imagine. Never mind that some of the blinds were thrown together 40 years ago and have experienced zero maintenance since then. There have been times when it seemed absolutely certain that if the lightning didn't strike it first, that the high winds would roll my blind (with me inside) across the pasture and through the woods. Also, you know the structure isn't too tight when every inside surface has water streaming down it.

During several such storms I was able to actually watch whitetails in the middle of the fury. At times they ran in terror from the lightning and thunder, but more commonly they just stood there, sometimes even continuing to eat. It seems that big bucks have nerves of steel during thunderstorms as well as any other time.

I must have sat, squatted, huddled or shivered in every kind of deer blind known to civilization. A couple were like the Taj Mahal, nice enough to live in. Most, on the other hand, have been some version of the ramshackle blinds previously described.

Whitetails are frequently seen around roads and fencerows, and those can be some of the best places to start looking for them. The road in the above photo went for miles through thick oak forests. I walked quietly down the winding road, stopping every two or three hundred yards to rattle. This buck ran right out into the middle of the road and did a double-take when he saw me. In an instant he was gone forever. The buck at the left is crossing the fence at a well used location.

Some of the rudest surprises associated with deer blinds can occur when you clean them out after a year of non-use, or even worse, when you crawl into one in the darkness that hasn't been cleaned out in a while. They frequently contain wasps, spiders, snakes, or scorpions — even an occasional ringtail cat, raccoon or owl. In some areas where I photograph, the blinds are invariably filled with the giant, harmless spiders we call "daddy longlegs." They may be harmless, but when there are great gobs of them crawling all over you, it is somewhat distracting. The black widows are more worrisome, and I've squashed my share of them. The scorpions and the wasps are insidious, because they tend to be hidden in the cracks of the blinds, only to emerge later during your stay. Then you have to try to avoid and/or exterminate them without frightening the deer.

Owls present a variety of problems where deer blinds are concerned. They frequently live in them during the off-season, filling them up with furballs, bones and owl poop. Once in a while, there is an owl inside the blind at the time of attempted entry, and that always makes for a fun time. Then, finally, you've just never really lived until a bird the size of a small pterodactyl actually flies into the blind with you during the pre-dawn hour. Holy smoke!

I have enough weather "war stories" to make a meteorologist jealous. On one

Any type of activity that opens up the woods and creates "edges" is a good place to find whitetails. Powerline right-of-ways and railroad right-of-ways are good examples.

Find the places where whitetails are feeding and many times you can figure out a way to get to them in conjunction with their feeding habits. It can work with food plots or with natural foods, such as the lichens that the buck at the bottom is eating.

notable trip I was alone on an isolated ranch and hadn't seen much whitetail activity. It had been unusually hot, and the deer seemed to be moving nocturnally. As night fell, I was keeping a close watch on the weather, since it appeared that a change was on the way. There was no house, so I was sleeping in my truck. After dark I was still hot and dirty from a long, hard day, so I drove to the only water source on the ranch, a windmill, to take a shower under the spigot. After I got cleaned up, it was lightning heavily to the west, and the wind was picking up, so I decided to head out to the back pasture before the rain started. That was the area where I wanted to work the next morning, and there was a crossing on the way that would not be passable after a hard rain. If I went to the back pasture before the rain came, I would be there in the morning and be able to walk to the blind, rain or shine.

I guess it was just meant to be "one of those days." I had several miles of bad roads to cover in the darkness. About halfway there, I could actually hear the hissing as air began escaping from my left rear tire. I had to keep going until I could get to a place level enough to change a flat tire. It wouldn't have been such a big deal if the truck hadn't slipped off the jack with the wheel off, leaving the hub on the ground and the axle-jack all but worthless. I eventually worked it all out by about midnight and got back into the truck just before the downpour began. I pulled into the downwind side of a clump of oak trees and tried to settle in for the night.

I've never ridden out such a storm in my life! And it lasted virtually all night. The wind rocked the truck so hard that it was impossible to sleep, and there was an incredible electrical storm. I was almost certain that the high winds were going to roll the truck, but for some reason it didn't go over. I felt truly alone in the world for those few hours. There was no sleep, but, as luck would have it, the heavy rain ceased just before daybreak. I put on my boots and slogged across the pasture to a deer blind. Between the ankle-deep mud and the heavy load of equipment, it wasn't very easy. To my amazement I saw deer like I've never seen on that place, either before or since. The fury of the storm had made it impossible for the deer to move and feed during the night, and every deer in the

Watering places can be good locations to find deer, although many times deer travel to water under cover of darkness. They're found in association with water more frequently during warm weather. Always keep in mind that a whitetail buck may show up just about anywhere ...even in the middle of a prickly pear clump.

I really enjoy going into the thick stuff after whitetails, particularly if I can find a creek or ravine to follow. The photos on this page are examples of the view from the inside out. I like to get in the middle of the cover and watch the whitetails as they work the edges of it. They are generally watching for danger from the other direction, and it offers some unique perspectives.

country was on the move. I saw at least 20 different bucks that morning in a place where I might normally *hope* to see only two or three. Extreme weather can certainly have extreme effects on whitetail movement. I've seen other similar examples of such phenomena since then.

There are times when it can be advantageous to sleep in a truck or a blind in order to be in the right place the next morning with a minimum of disturbance. It's paid off for me on several occasions. Even when I'm not planning to stay overnight in a blind, I'll sometimes remain there until 10 or 11 p.m. if there is a full or

bright moon. At times, particularly during warm weather, there just isn't much movement until after dark. If it's light enough to see with binoculars by moonlight, I may stay awhile just to take inventory, to see what will show up that might be worth waiting for in the near future. I've seen some real surprises!

I remember one particularly interesting experience. I arrived at a ranch late in the day and was making a quick drive through one of the pastures to see what I could find before dark. A huge drop-tine buck and another deer ran across the road 50 yards in front of me. I backtracked to see where they had come from. It appeared that they had been in a 10-acre oat patch and had traveled across a brushy hill to get to the road. By flashlight, I analyzed the trails coming out of the field. I made my best guess as to the primary trail and parked my truck parallel to it in the brush about 40 yards away. I got out and scattered corn along the trail in the spots where I figured the morning sun would be shining.

The use of decoys is very effective. A wide range of setups can be used successfully, depending on the situation. Overall, visibility is the key. As you can see, decoys work well as does, bucks or even as a dual setup. Bucks are always curious and frequently confused by them. Some bucks fall in love with them, and others show them no mercy as they thrash them furiously.

The whitetails are jumping, adrenaline pumping
Survival's just part of the game
Such leaps are amazing, their quickness is blazing
It's led to their fortune and fame

Deer antlers attract us, buck fever attacks us
Close encounters leave folks feeling numb
We think that we've got them, it turns out it's not them
But it's us that's been beat like a drum

We've been there before, and we'll go back for more
Sweet success always seems so near
We'll take the abuses, and make our excuses
If we just get to dance with the deer

..... Mike Biggs